Home, School, and Community Relations

Join us on the web at

www.cengage.com/education

Home, School, and Community Relations

Carol Gestwicki

DELMAR
CENGAGE Learning

Australia • Brazil • Japan • Korea • Mexico • Singapore • Spain • United Kingdom • United States

OUACHITA TECHNICAL COLLEGE

**Home, School, and
Community Relations**
Carol Gestwicki

For product information and technology assistance, contact us at
Cengage Learning Customer & Sales Support, 1-800-354-9706
For permission to use material from this text or product, submit all requests online at
www.cengage.com/permissions
Further permissions questions can be e-mailed to
permissionrequest@cengage.com

Library of Congress Catalog Card Number: 2006011904

ISBN-13: 978-1-4180-2984-5
ISBN-10: 1-4180-2984-X

Delmar
10 Davis Drive
Belmont, CA 94002-3098
USA

Cengage Learning is a leading provider of customized learning solutions with office locations around the globe, including Singapore, the United Kingdom, Australia, Mexico, Brazil, and Japan. Locate your local office at:
www.cengage.com/global

Cengage Learning products are represented in Canada by Nelson Education, Ltd.

To learn more about Delmar, visit
www.cengage.com/delmar

Purchase any of our products at your local college store or at our preferred online store
www.ichapters.com

Printed in the United States of America
5 6 7 8 9 10 11 10 09 08

TABLE OF CONTENTS

This tool was developed to help you, the budding teacher and/or child care provider, as you move into your first classroom. The editors at Cengage Learning encourage and appreciate your feedback on this or any of our other products. Go to www.cengage.com/education and click on the Contact Us link.

INTRODUCTION

Throughout a college program of preparation to become an early childhood educator, students take many courses and read many textbooks. Their knowledge grows, as they accumulate ideas from lectures, reading, experiences, and discussions. When they finish their coursework, graduate, and move into their first teaching positions, students often leave behind some of the books they have used. The hope is, however, that they will take with them the important ideas from their classes and books as they begin their own professional practice.

More experienced colleagues or mentors sometimes support teachers in their first teaching positions, helping them make the transition between college classroom and being responsible for a group of young children. Other times, new teachers are left to travel their own paths, relying on their own resources. Whatever your situation, this professional enhancement guide is designed to provide reminders of what you have learned, as well as resources to help you make sense of and apply that knowledge.

Teachers of young children are under great pressure today. From families, there are the demands for support in their difficult tasks of child-rearing in today's fast-paced and changing world. Some families become so overwhelmed with the tasks of parenting that they seem to leave too much responsibility on the shoulders of teachers and caregivers. From administrators and institutions, there are expectations that sometimes seem overwhelming. Teachers are being held accountable for children's learning in ways unprecedented in even the recent past. Public scrutiny has led to insistence on teaching practices that may seem contrary to the best interests of children or their teachers. New teachers may find themselves caught between the realities of the schools or centers where they find themselves, and their own philosophies and ideals of working with children. When faced with such dilemmas, it is important for these individuals to be able to fall back and reflect on what they know of best practices, renewing their professional determination to make appropriate decisions for children.

These books provide similar tools for that reflection:

- tips for getting off to a great start in your new environment
- information about typical developmental patterns of children from birth through school age
- suggestions for materials that promote development for children from infancy through the primary grades
- tools to assist teachers in observing children and gathering data to help set appropriate goals for individual children
- guides for planning appropriate classroom experiences and sample lesson plans
- tips for introducing children to the joys of literacy
- a summary of the key ideas about Developmentally Appropriate Practice, the process of decision making that allows teachers to provide optimum environments for children from birth through school age, and of the ideas particularly related to working with families
- resources for teachers for professional development
- ideas for where you can access lists of other resources
- case studies of relevant, realistic situations you may face, as well as best practices for successfully navigating them
- insight into issues and trends facing early childhood educators today

Becoming a teacher is a process of continuing to grow, learn, reflect, and discover through experience. Having these resources may help you along your way. Good luck on your journey!

REFLECTIONS FOR GROWING TEACHERS

Teachers spend most of their time working with young children and their families. During the day, questions and concerns arise and decisions have to be made, meaning teachers must always be reflective about their work. Too often, teachers believe they are too busy to spend time thinking, but experienced professional teachers have learned that reflection sustains their best work. Growing teachers need to regularly take time to consider the questions and concerns that arise from their practice. Some teachers use journals to keep track of the process.

Use these questions to begin your reflection and then add to them with questions from your own experience. Remember, these are not questions to be answered once and forgotten: Come back often. Reflection is a skill that takes practice; make opportunities for reflective thinking part of your daily routine as a teacher.

QUESTIONS FOR REFLECTION

(Adapted from Nilsen, B. A., *Week by Week: Documenting the Development of Young Children,* 3E, published by Cengage Learning.)

This day would have been better if _____

_____

I think I need to know more about _____

_____

One new thing I think I'll try this week is _____

_____

The highlight of this week was_____

_____

The observations this week made me think more about _____

_____

I think my favorite creative activity this year was _____

_____

One area where my teaching is changing is _____

_____

One area where my teaching needs to change is _____

_____

One of my strengths in working with families is _____

_____

One of the areas I need to work on in working with families is _____

_____

I just don't understand why _____

_____

I loved my job this week when _____

_____

I hated my job this week when _____

_____

One thing I can try to make better next week is _____

_____

The funniest thing I heard a child say this week was _____

_____

The family member I feel most comfortable with is_____

And I think the reason for that is _____

_____

The family member I feel least comfortable with is _____

And I think the reason for that is _____

_____

One of the ways I prefer to communicate with families is _____

_____

I think I should try this in communicating with families _____

_____

The biggest gains in learning have been made by _____

_____

And I think that this is because _____

_____

I'm working on a bad habit of _____

_____

Has my attitude about working with families changed this year? Why? _____

_____

What have I done lately to spark the children's imagination and creativity? _____

_____

One quote that I like to keep in mind is _____

_____

Dealing with _____ is the most difficult thing I had to face recently

because _____

My teaching style has been most influenced by _____

_____

In thinking more about including families in my curriculum, I believe _____

_____

In thinking more about including understandings of diversity in my curriculum,

I believe _____

If I were going to advise a new teacher, the most helpful piece of advice would be

_____

I've been trying to facilitate friendships among the children by _____

_____

I really need to start _____

_____

I used to _____ but now I _____

_____

The child who has helped me learn the most is _____

I learned _____

I've grown in my communication by _____

_____

The best thing I've learned by observing is _____

_____

I still don't understand why _____

_____

One mistake I used to make that I don't make any longer is _____

_____

When next year starts, one thing I will do more of is _____

_____

When next year starts, one thing I won't do is_____

_____

One way I can help my children feel more competent is_____

_____

Something I enjoy that I could share with my class is _____

_____

When children have difficulty sharing, I _____

_____

One thing that has been helpful for me to remember about working with families is

_____

_____

_____

_____

_____

_____

_____

_____

_____

_____

TIPS FOR SUCCESS

Remember that you are a role model for the children. They are constantly watching how you dress, what you say, and what you do. It is important that you use your knowledge and studies of children and families in all that you do. In addition, these practical tips may help.

BE A PROFESSIONAL

- Dress conservatively and follow your employer's clothing expectations (which could include wearing closed-toe shoes to be safe and active with children and wearing clean, modest, and comfortable clothing).

- Be prepared and on time.

- Avoid excessive absences.

- Use appropriate language with children and adults.

- Be positive when talking to parents and show that you are forming a positive relationship with their child; "catch children doing something right" and share those accomplishments. Challenges with children can be discussed after you have established trust with the parents.

- Remember that working with every family is an important teaching role.

BE A TEAM PLAYER

- Rely on team members to help you learn the parameters of your new position.

- Don't be afraid to ask questions or for guidance from teammates.

- Show your support and be responsible.

- Step in to do your share of the work; don't expect others to clean up after you.

- Be of assistance to others whenever possible.

- Respect others' ideas and avoid telling them how to do things.

- Strive to balance your ability to make decisions with following the lead of others.

LEARN ABOUT CHILDREN

- Apply what you have learned about children's development physically, socially, emotionally, and cognitively.

- Assess children's development and plan curriculum that will enhance it.

- Remember that children will test you! (Children, especially school age, will expect that you don't know the rules and may try to convince you to let them do things that were not previously allowed.)

- Never hesitate to double-check something with teammates when in doubt.

- Use positive guidance techniques with children.

- Recognize and respect family values and cultural influences for every child.

GUIDANCE TECHNIQUES FOR GAINING CHILDREN'S COOPERATION

There are myriad techniques that will help children cooperate. Children need respectful reminders of expectations and adult support in performing to those expectations. Be sure that your expectations are age appropriate and individually appropriate. These techniques are more preventive in nature. Remember to:

- Use positive phrases and state exactly what you expect children to do. "Stand by the door" is more effective than "Don't go outside until everyone is ready."

- Avoid "no" and "don't." Be clear about what it is you want children to do, not what you don't want them to do.

- Sequence directions using "When-then." For example, "When things are put away where they belong, then we can go outside."

- Stay close. Merely standing near children can be enough to help them manage behavior. Be aware, however, that if you are talking to another adult, children may act out because they know they do not have your attention.

- Offer sufficient and appropriate choices. Children need a variety of activities that interest them and that will create opportunities for success.

- Create a schedule that balances children's activity with quieter periods to help children retain control.

- Communicate with families about changes or stresses in their children's lives.

- Communicate with families about their guidance strategies at home, remembering that guidance is a complex topic, about which there is no one right answer.

GETTING OFF TO A GOOD START

Remember that working with families to help their children become comfortable in a new classroom setting is a critical part of beginning a partnership. Sometimes both young children and their parents experience separation difficulties, and support at the beginning is important to establishing trust and communication. Teachers help when they:

- Give parents much information, both written and oral, about classroom routines and expectations.

- Use the school's questionnaire (or devise one) to allow parents to give specific information about their child.

- Help parents understand separation anxiety and possible behaviors in advance, as well as giving them information on what they can do to help their children. The handout on the next page could be copied and given to families.

- Make opportunities for visits and easing-in before children participate fully in the program.

- Offer explanations about children's possible responses when parents return.

- Encourage families to understand that transitions and separations are important learning for children, and will take patience and understanding.

- Communicate regularly with families, to provide information about children's adjustment, and hear how it is going from parents' perspective. Extra time and attention in the beginning to both children and their parents will pay off in comfort and positive working relationships.

HANDOUT FOR BEGINNING FAMILIES

We know that you want to help your child get off to a good start in beginning school. Young children often experience difficulties with separation from their significant adults in new situations. They may cry or cling, or behave differently than you are used to. Be assured that this is a typical, normal response, and that these behaviors will slowly stop as children (and you) get more comfortable with the new situation. Some things you could do to support your child at this time are:

- Accept and respect your child's temporary unhappiness. Say things like "I know you're feeling sad when Dad leaves, but you will have a good time, and soon you won't be so sad."

- Give yourselves enough time in the morning. Children often get anxious when rushed.

- Have pleasant conversation as you learn about some of the things your child enjoys about preschool.

- Remind your child of the predictability of your pick-up arrangements, tying your return with an event, such as after naptime, and then arrive when you have said.

- Establish a pattern of what you will each do when you enter the classroom each day.

- Encourage your child to do as much as she can independently during the arrival process; for example, if your child is old enough, walking into the classroom herself.

- If you can stay for 3 or 4 minutes, help your child find an activity to focus on.

- After you have said you will go, make your good-bye prompt, affectionate, and positive. Don't ever be tempted to sneak away while your child is occupied.

- Have your child's teacher step in to help with good-byes when you give the sign that you're ready to go.

- Avoid the temptation to pressure your child not to cry or to offer bribes for "good behavior." Learning to cope with sadness is important learning for your child.

- Let the teacher know if there are particular routines or objects that bring comfort to your child. The teacher will be helped by this knowledge.

- Understand that the process of learning to trust new people naturally takes time. The teacher will be glad to discuss your concerns with you—together you can make plans to meet your child's needs.

GETTING STARTED

There is always an array of information to learn when starting in a new position working with children. Use this fill-in-the-blank section to customize this resource book to your specific environment.

What are the school's or center's hours of operation?

On school days: _____

_____

_____

On vacation days: _____

_____

_____

What is the basic daily schedule and what are my responsibilities during each time segment?

_____

_____

_____

_____

_____

_____

What are the procedures for checking children in and out of the program? Are there assignments made for communicating with families?

_____

_____

Do I call if I have to be absent? Who is my contact?

Name: _____

Phone Number: _____

What is the dress code for employees?

_____

_____

For what basic health and safety practices will I be responsible? Where are the materials stored for this? (Bleach, gloves, etc.)

Sanitizing tables: _____

_____

Cleaning and maintaining of equipment and materials: _____

_____

_____

What are the emergency procedures?

Mildly injured child: _____

_____

_____

_____

Earthquake/Tornado: _____

_____

_____

_____

Fire: _____

_____

_____

_____

First Aid: _____

_____

_____

_____

Other: _____

_____

_____

_____

COMMUNICATION WITH FAMILIES

What methods are used regularly for communication with families?

What are my responsibilities for communication?

What is the procedure for unusual family requests? For cases of conflict?

DEVELOPMENTAL MILESTONES BY AGE

(Some content in this section adapted from Allen, E. A., & Marotz, L.,
Developmental Profiles: Pre-birth through Twelve, 4E, published by Cengage Learning.)

Whether you are working with infants, toddlers, preschoolers, or primary-aged children, a teacher's first requirement is to have knowledge about how children develop and learn. In your college program, you no doubt studied child development. The following is a shortened version of the universal steps most children go through as they develop. Some children will move easily from one step to another, while other children move forward in one area but lag behind in others. Use these milestones as a guide for arranging an environment and planning activities in your room. Share these milestones with families as well.

DEVELOPMENTAL CHECKLIST

Child's Name _____ Age _____

Observer _____ Date _____

BY SIX MONTHS:	Yes	No	Sometimes
Does the child . . .			
Show continued gains in height, weight, and head circumference?			
Reach for toys or objects when they are presented?			
Begin to roll from stomach to back?			
Sit with minimal support?			
Transfer objects from one hand to the other?			
Rise up on arms, lifting head and chest, when placed on stomach?			
Babble, coo, and imitate sounds?			
Turn to locate the source of a sound?			
Focus on an object and follow its movement vertically and horizontally?			
Exhibit a blink reflex?			
Enjoy being held and cuddled?			
Recognize and respond to familiar faces?			
Begin sleeping six to eight hours through the night?			
Suck vigorously when it is time to eat?			
Enjoy playing in water during bath time?			

Developmental Alerts

Check with a health care provider or early childhood specialist if, by one month of age, the infant *does not:*

- Show alarm or "startle" responses to loud noise.
- Suck and swallow with ease.
- Show gains in height, weight, and head circumference.
- Grasp with equal strength with both hands.
- Make eye-to-eye contact when awake and being held.
- Become quiet soon after being picked up.
- Roll head from side to side when placed on stomach.
- Express needs and emotions with cries and patterns of vocalizations that can be distinguished from one another.
- Stop crying when picked up and held.

Developmental Alerts

Check with a health care provider or early childhood specialist if, by four months of age, the infant *does not:*

- Continue to show steady increases in height, weight, and head circumference.
- Smile in response to the smiles of others (the social smile is a significant developmental milestone).
- Follow a moving object with eyes focusing together.
- Bring hands together over mid-chest.
- Turn head to locate sounds.
- Begin to raise head and upper body when placed on stomach.
- Reach for objects or familiar persons.

DEVELOPMENTAL CHECKLIST

Child's Name _____ Age _____

Observer _____ Date _____

BY TWELVE MONTHS:	Yes	No	Sometimes
Does the child . . .			
Walk with assistance?			
Roll a ball in imitation of an adult?			
Pick objects up with thumb and forefinger?			
Transfer objects from one hand to the other?			
Pick up dropped toys?			
Look directly at adult's face?			
Imitate gestures: peek-a-boo, bye-bye, pat-a-cake?			
Find object hidden under a cup?			
Feed self crackers (munching, not sucking on them)?			
Hold cup with two hands; drink with assistance?			
Smile spontaneously?			
Pay attention to own name?			
Respond to "no"?			
Respond differently to strangers and familiar persons?			
Respond differently to sounds: vacuum, phone, door?			
Look at person who speaks to him or her?			
Respond to simple directions accompanied by gestures?			
Make several consonant–vowel combination sounds?			
Vocalize back to person who has talked to him or her?			
Use intonation patterns that sound like scolding, asking, exclaiming?			
Say "da-da" or "ma-ma"?			

Developmental Alerts

Check with a health care provider or early childhood specialist if, by twelve months of age, the infant *does not:*

■ Blink when fast-moving objects approach the eyes.

■ Begin to cut teeth.

- Imitate simple sounds.
- Follow simple verbal requests: *come, bye-bye.*
- Pull self to a standing position.

DEVELOPMENTAL CHECKLIST

Child's Name _____   Age _____
Observer _____   Date _____

BY TWO YEARS:	Yes	No	Sometimes
Does the child . . .			
Walk alone?			
Bend over and pick up toy without falling over?			
Seat self in child-size chair? Walk up and down stairs with assistance?			
Place several rings on a stick?			
Place five pegs in a pegboard?			
Turn pages two or three at a time?			
Scribble?			
Follow one-step direction involving something familiar: "Give me _____." "Show me _____." "Get a _____."?			
Match familiar objects?			
Use spoon with some spilling?			
Drink from cup holding it with one hand, unassisted?			
Chew food?			
Take off coat, shoe, sock?			
Zip and unzip large zipper?			
Recognize self in mirror or picture?			
Refer to self by name?			
Imitate adult behaviors in play—for example, feeds "baby"?			
Help put things away?			
Respond to specific words by showing what was named: toy, pet, family member?			
Ask for desired items by name: (cookie)?			
Answer with name of object when asked "What's that"?			
Make some two-word statements: "Daddy bye-bye"?			

Developmental Alerts

Check with a health care provider or early childhood specialist if, by twenty-four months of age, the child *does not:*

- Attempt to talk or repeat words.

- Understand some new words.

- Respond to simple questions with "yes" or "no."

- Walk alone (or with very little help).

- Exhibit a variety of emotions: anger, delight, fear.

- Show interest in pictures.

- Recognize self in mirror.

- Attempt self-feeding: hold own cup to mouth and drink.

DEVELOPMENTAL CHECKLIST

Child's Name _____ Age _____

Observer _____ Date _____

BY THREE YEARS:	Yes	No	Sometimes
Does the child . . .			
Run well in a forward direction?			
Jump in place, two feet together?			
Walk on tiptoe?			
Throw ball (but without direction or aim)?			
Kick ball forward?			
String four large beads?			
Turn pages in book singly?			
Hold crayon: imitate circular, vertical, horizontal strokes?			
Match shapes?			
Demonstrate number concepts of 1 and 2? (Can select 1 or 2; can tell if one or two objects.)			
Use spoon without spilling?			
Drink from a straw?			
Put on and take off coat?			

BY THREE YEARS:	Yes	No	Sometimes
Wash and dry hands with some assistance?			
Watch other children; play near them; sometimes join in their play?			
Defend own possessions?			
Use symbols in play—for example, tin pan on head becomes helmet and crate becomes a spaceship?			
Respond to "Put _____ in the box," "Take the _____ out of the box"?			
Select correct item on request: big versus little; one versus two?			
Identify objects by their use: show own shoe when asked, "What do you wear on your feet?"			
Ask questions?			
Tell about something with functional phrases that carry meaning: "Daddy go airplane."			
"Me hungry now"?			

Developmental Alerts

Check with a health care provider or early childhood specialist if, by the third birthday, the child *does not:*

- Eat a fairly well-rounded diet, even though amounts are limited.

- Walk confidently with few stumbles or falls; climb steps with help.

- Avoid bumping into objects.

- Carry out simple, two-step directions: "Come to Daddy and bring your book"; express desires; ask questions.

- Point to and name familiar objects; use two- or three-word sentences.

- Enjoy being read to.

- Show interest in playing with other children: watching, perhaps imitating.

- Indicate a beginning interest in toilet training.

- Sort familiar objects according to a single characteristic, such as type, color, or size.

DEVELOPMENTAL CHECKLIST

Child's Name _____ Age _____

Observer _____ Date _____

BY FOUR YEARS:	Yes	No	Sometimes
Does the child . . .			
Walk on a line?			
Balance on one foot briefly? Hop on one foot?			
Jump over an object 6 inches high and land on both feet together?			
Throw ball with direction?			
Copy circles and *X*'s?			
Match six colors?			
Count to 5?			
Pour well from pitcher? Spread butter, jam with knife?			
Button, unbutton large buttons?			
Know own sex, age, last name?			
Use toilet independently and reliably?			
Wash and dry hands unassisted?			
Listen to stories for at least 5 minutes?			
Draw head of person and at least one other body part?			
Play with other children?			
Share, take turns (with some assistance)?			
Engage in dramatic and pretend play?			
Respond appropriately to "Put it beside," "Put it under"?			
Respond to two-step directions: "Give me the sweater and put the shoe on the floor"?			
Respond by selecting the correct object—for example, hard versus soft object?			
Answer "if," "what," and "when" questions?			
Answer questions about function: "What are books for"?			

Developmental Alerts

Check with a health care provider or early childhood specialist if, by the fourth birthday, the child *does not:*

- Have intelligible speech most of the time; have children's hearing checked if there is any reason for concern.

- Understand and follow simple commands and directions.

- State own name and age.

- Enjoy playing near or with other children.

- Use three- to four-word sentences.

- Ask questions.

- Stay with an activity for 3 or 4 minutes; play alone several minutes at a time.

- Jump in place without falling.

- Balance on one foot, at least briefly.

- Help with dressing self.

Five- to Seven-Year-Olds

- More independent of parents, able to take care of their own physical needs.

- Rely upon their peer group for self-esteem, have two or three best friends.

- Learn to share and take turns, participate in group games.

- Are eager to learn and succeed in school.

- Have a sense of duty and develop a conscience.

- Are less aggressive and resolve conflicts with words.

- Begin to see others' point of view.

- Can sustain interest for long periods of time.

- Can remember and relate past events.

- Have good muscle control and can manage simple tools.

- Have a high energy level.

DEVELOPMENTAL CHECKLIST

Child's Name _____   Age _____

Observer _____   Date _____

BY FIVE YEARS:	Yes	No	Sometimes
Does the child . . .			
Walk backward, heel to toe?			
Walk up and down stairs, alternating feet?			
Cut on line?			
Print some letters?			
Point to and name three shapes?			
Group common related objects: shoe, sock, and foot: apple, orange, and plum?			
Demonstrate number concepts to 4 or 5?			
Cut food with a knife: celery, sandwich?			
Lace shoes?			
Read from story picture book—in other words, tell story by looking at pictures?			
Draw a person with three to six body parts?			
Play and interact with other children; engage in dramatic play that is close to reality?			
Build complex structures with blocks or other building materials?			
Respond to simple three-step directions: "Give me the pencil, put the book on the table, and hold the comb in your hand"?			
Respond correctly when asked to show penny, nickel, and dime?			
Ask "How" questions?			
Respond verbally to "Hi" and "How are you"?			
Tell about event using past and future tenses?			
Use conjunctions to string words and phrases together—for example, "I saw a bear and a zebra and a giraffe at the zoo"?			

Developmental Alerts

Check with a health care provider or early childhood specialist if, by the fifth birthday, the child *does not*:

- State own name in full.

- Recognize simple shapes: circle, square, triangle.

- Catch a large ball when bounced (have child's vision checked).

- Speak so as to be understood by strangers (have child's hearing checked).

- Have good control of posture and movement.

- Hop on one foot.

- Appear interested in, and responsive to, surroundings.

- Respond to statements without constantly asking to have them repeated.

- Dress self with minimal adult assistance; manage buttons, zippers.

- Take care of own toilet needs; have good bowel and bladder control with infrequent accidents.

DEVELOPMENTAL CHECKLIST

Child's Name _____   Age _____

Observer _____   Date _____

BY SIX YEARS: Does the child . . .	Yes	No	Sometimes
Walk across a balance beam?			
Skip with alternating feet?			
Hop for several seconds on one foot?			
Cut out simple shapes?			
Copy own first name?			
Show well-established handedness; demonstrate consistent right- or left-handedness?			
Sort objects on one or more dimensions: color, shape, or function?			
Name most letters and numerals?			
Count by rote to 10; know what number comes next?			
Dress self completely; tie bows?			
Brush teeth unassisted?			
Have some concept of clock time in relation to daily schedule?			

(continues on next page)

BY SIX YEARS:	Yes	No	Sometimes
Cross street safely?			
Draw a person with head, trunk, legs, arms, and features; often add clothing details?			
Play simple board games?			
Engage in cooperative play with other children, involving group decisions, role assignments, rule observance?			
Use construction toys, such as Legos, blocks, to make recognizable structures?			
Do fifteen-piece puzzles?			
Use all grammatical structures: pronouns, plurals, verb tenses, conjunctions?			
Use complex sentences: carry on conversations?			

Developmental Alerts

Check with a health care provider or early childhood specialist if, by the sixth birthday, the child *does not:*

- Alternate feet when walking up and down stairs.

- Speak in a moderate voice; neither too loud, too soft, too high, too low.

- Follow simple directions in stated order: "Please go to the cupboard, get a cup, and bring it to me.

- Use four to five words in acceptable sentence structure.

- Cut on a line with scissors.

- Sit still and listen to an entire short story (five to seven minutes).

- Maintain eye contact when spoken to (unless this is a cultural taboo).

- Play well with other children.

- Perform most self-grooming tasks independently: brush teeth, wash hands and face.

DEVELOPMENTAL CHECKLIST

Child's Name _____   Age _____
Observer _____   Date _____

BY SEVEN YEARS:	Yes	No	Sometimes
Does the child . . .			
Concentrate on completing puzzles and board games?			
Ask many questions?			
Use correct verb tenses, word order, and sentence structure in conversation?			
Correctly identify right and left hands?			
Make friends easily?			
Show some control of anger, using words instead of physical aggression?			
Participate in play that requires teamwork and rule observance?			
Seek adult approval for efforts?			
Enjoy reading and being read to?			
Use pencil to write words and numbers?			
Sleep undisturbed through the night?			
Catch a tennis ball, walk across balance beam, hit ball with bat?			
Plan and carry out simple projects with minimal adult help?			
Tie own shoes?			
Draw pictures with greater detail and sense of proportion?			
Care for own personal needs with some adult supervision? Wash hands? Brush teeth? Use toilet? Dress self?			
Show some understanding of cause-and-effect concepts?			

Developmental Alerts

Check with a health care provider or early childhood specialist if, by the seventh birthday, the child *does not:*

- Show signs of ongoing growth: increasing height and weight; continuing motor development, such as running, jumping, balancing.

- Show some interest in reading and trying to reproduce letters, especially own name.

- Follow simple, multiple-step directions: "Finish your book, put it on the shelf, and then get your coat on."

- Follow through with instructions and complete simple tasks: putting dishes in the sink, picking up clothes, finishing a puzzle. *Note:* All children forget. Task incompletion is not a problem unless a child *repeatedly* leaves tasks unfinished.

- Begin to develop alternatives to excessive use of inappropriate behaviors in order to get own way.

- Develop a steady decrease in tension-type behaviors that may have developed with starting school: repeated grimacing or facial tics; eye twitching; grinding of teeth; regressive soiling or wetting; frequent stomachaches; refusing to go to school.

Eight- to Ten-Year-Olds

- Need parental guidance and support for school achievement.

- Competition is common.

- Pronounced gender differences in interests, same gender cliques formed.

- Spend a lot of time in physical game playing.

- Academic achievement is important.

- Begin to develop moral values, make value judgments about own behavior.

- Are aware of the importance of belonging.

- Strong gender role conformation.

- Begin to think logically and to understand cause and effect.

- Use language to communicate ideas and can use abstract words.

- Can read but ability varies.

- Realize importance of physical skills in determining status among peers.

DEVELOPMENTAL CHECKLIST

Child's Name _____   Age _____

Observer _____   Date _____

BY EIGHT AND NINE YEARS:	Yes	No	Sometimes
Does the child . . .			
Have energy to play, continuing growth, few illnesses?			
Use pencil in a deliberate and controlled manner?			
Express relatively complex thoughts in a clear and logical fashion?			
Carry out multiple four- to five-step instructions?			
Become less easily frustrated with own performance?			
Interact and play cooperatively with other children?			
Show interest in creative expression—telling stories, jokes, writing, drawing, singing?			
Use eating utensils with ease?			
Have a good appetite? Show interest in trying new foods?			
Know how to tell time?			
Have control of bowel and bladder functions?			
Participate in some group activities—games, sports, plays?			
Want to go to school? Seem disappointed if must miss a day?			
Demonstrate beginning skills in reading, writing, and math?			
Accept responsibility and complete work independently?			
Handle stressful situations without becoming overly upset?			

Developmental Alerts

Check with a health care provider or early childhood specialist if, by the eighth birthday, the child *does not:*

- Attend to the task at hand; show longer periods of sitting quietly, listening, responding appropriately.

- Follow through on simple instructions.

- Go to school willingly most days (of concern are excessive complaints about stomachaches or headaches when getting ready for school).

- Make friends (observe closely to see if the child plays alone most of the time or withdraws consistently from contact with other children).

- Sleep soundly most nights (frequent and recurring nightmares or bad dreams are usually at a minimum at this age).

- Seem to see or hear adequately at times (squints, rubs eyes excessively, asks frequently to have things repeated).

- Handle stressful situations without undue emotional upset (excessive crying, sleeping or eating disturbances, withdrawal, frequent anxiety).

- Assume responsibility for personal care (dressing, bathing, feeding self) most of the time.

- Show improved motor skills.

Developmental Alerts

Check with a health care provider or early childhood specialist if, by the ninth birthday, the child *does not:*

- Exhibit a good appetite and continued weight gain (some children, especially girls, may already begin to show early signs of an eating disorder).

- Experience fewer illnesses.

- Show improved motor skills, in terms of agility, speed, and balance.

- Understand abstract concepts and use complex thought processes to problem-solve.

- Enjoy school and the challenge of learning.

- Follow through on multiple-step instructions.

- Express ideas clearly and fluently.

- Form friendships with other children and enjoy participating in group activities.

Eleven- to Twelve-Year-Olds

- Parental influence is decreasing and some rebellion may occur.

- Peer group is important and sets standards for behavior.

- Worry about what others think.

- Choose friends based on common interests.

- Gender differences in interests.

- Develop awareness and interest in opposite gender.

- Begin to question adult authority.

- Often reluctant to attend child care; are bored or think they can care for themselves.

- May be moody and experience stress over physical changes of puberty.

- May be rebellious as they seek their own identity.

- Can think abstractly and apply logic to solving problems.

- Have a good command of spoken and written language.

- Girls develop gender characteristics, boys begin a growth spurt.

- Early maturing is related to a positive self-image.

- Able to master physical skills necessary for playing games.

DEVELOPMENTAL CHECKLIST

Child's Name _____ Age _____
Observer _____ Date _____

BY TEN AND ELEVEN YEARS:	Yes	No	Sometimes
Does the child . . .			
Continue to increase in height and weight?			
Exhibit improving coordination: running, climbing, riding a bike, writing?			
Handle stressful situations without becoming overly upset or violent?			
Construct sentences using reasonably correct grammar: nouns, adverbs, verbs, adjectives?			
Understand concepts of time, distance, space, volume?			
Have one or two "best friends"?			
Maintain friendships over time?			
Approach challenges with a reasonable degree of self-confidence?			
Play cooperatively and follow group instructions?			
Begin to show an understanding of moral standards: right from wrong, fairness, honesty, good from bad?			
Look forward to, and enjoy, school?			
Appear to hear well and listen attentively?			
Enjoy reasonably good health, with few episodes of illness or health-related complaints?			
Have a good appetite and enjoy mealtimes?			
Take care of own personal hygiene without assistance?			
Sleep through the night, waking up refreshed and energetic?			

Developmental Alerts

Check with a health care provider or early childhood specialist if, by the eleventh birthday, the child *does not:*

- Continue to grow at a rate appropriate for the child's gender.

- Show continued improvement of fine motor skills.

- Make or keep friends.

- Enjoy going to school and show interest in learning (have children's hearing and vision tested; vision and hearing problems affect children's ability to learn and their interest in learning).

- Approach new situations with reasonable confidence.

- Handle failure and frustration in a constructive manner.

- Sleep through the night or experiences prolonged problems with bedwetting, nightmares, or sleepwalking.

DEVELOPMENTAL CHECKLIST

Child's Name _____ Age _____
Observer _____ Date _____

BY TWELVE YEARS:	Yes	No	Sometimes
Does the child . . .			
Appear to be growing: increasing height and maintaining a healthy weight (not too thin or too heavy)?			
Understand changes associated with puberty or have an opportunity to learn and ask questions?			
Complain of headaches or blurred vision?			
Have an abnormal posture or curving of the spine?			
Seem energetic and not chronically fatigued?			
Stay focused on a task and complete assignments?			
Remember and carry out complex instructions?			
Sequence, order, and classify objects?			
Use longer and more complex sentence structure?			
Engage in conversation; tell jokes and riddles?			
Enjoy playing organized games and team sports?			
Respond to anger-invoking situations without resorting to violence or physical aggression?			
Begin to understand and solve complex mathematical problems?			
Accept blame for actions on most occasions?			
Enjoy competition?			
Accept and carry out responsibility in a dependable manner?			
Go to bed willingly and wake up refreshed?			
Take pride in appearance; keep self reasonably clean?			

Developmental Alerts

Check with a health care provider or early childhood specialist if, by the thirteenth birthday, the child *does not*:

- Have movements that are smooth and coordinated.

- Have energy sufficient for playing, riding bikes, or engaging in other desired activities.

- Stay focused on tasks at hand.

- Understand basic cause-and-effect relationships.

- Handle criticism and frustration with a reasonable response (physical aggression and excessive crying could be an indication of other, underlying problems).

- Exhibit a healthy appetite (frequent skipping of meals is not typical for this age group).

- Make and keep friends.

DEVELOPMENTAL MILESTONES BY SKILL

(Some content in this section adapted from Allen, E. A., & Marotz, L., *Developmental Profiles: Pre-birth through Twelve*, 4E, published by Cengage Learning.)

As with the list of milestones by age, this list is not exhaustive, but it can be used to arrange an environment, to plan activities in your room, or to discuss developmental progress during conferences with parents.

BIRTH TO ONE MONTH

Physical	Date Observed
Engages in primarily reflexive motor activity	
Maintains "fetal" position especially when sleeping	
Holds hands in a fist; does not reach for objects	
In prone position, head falls lower than the body's horizontal line with hips flexed and arms and legs hanging down	
Has good upper body muscle tone when supported under the arms	
Cognitive	
Blinks in response to fast-approaching object	
Follows a slowly moving object through a complete 180-degree arc	
Follows objects moved vertically if close to infant's face	
Continues looking about, even in the dark	
Begins to study own hand when lying in tonic neck reflex position	
Prefers to listen to mother's voice rather than a stranger's	

(continues on next page)

BIRTH TO ONE MONTH (CONTINUED)

Language	Date Observed
Cries and fusses as major forms of communication	
Reacts to loud noises by blinking, moving (or stopping), shifting eyes, making a startle response	
Shows preference for certain sounds (music and human voices) by calming down or quieting	
Turns head to locate voices and other sounds	
Makes occasional sounds other than crying	
Social/Emotional	
Experiences a short period of alertness immediately following birth	
Sleeps 17–19 hours a day; is gradually awake and responsive for longer periods	
Likes to be held close and cuddled when awake	
Shows qualities of individuality in responding or not responding to similar situations	
Begins to establish emotional attachment or bonding with parents and caregivers	
Begins to develop a sense of security/trust with parents and caregivers; responses to different individuals vary	

ONE TO FOUR MONTHS

Physical	Date Observed
Rooting and sucking reflexes are well developed	
In prone position, Landau reflex appears and baby raises head and upper body on arms	
Grasps with entire hand; strength insufficient to hold items	
Movements tend to be large and jerky	
Turns head side to side when in a supine (face up) position	
Begins rolling from front to back by turning head to one side and allowing trunk to follow	
Cognitive	
Fixes on a moving object held at 12 inches (30.5 cm)	
Continues to gaze in direction of moving objects that have disappeared	
Exhibits some sense of size/color/shape recognition of objects in the immediate environment	

Cognitive	Date Observed
Alternates looking at an object, at one or both hands, and then back at the object	
Moves eyes from one object to another	
Focuses on small object and reaches for it; usually follows own hand movements	
Language	
Reacts to sounds (voice, rattle, doorbell); later will search for source by turning head	
Coordinates vocalizing, looking, and body movements in face-to-face exchanges with parent or caregiver	
Babbles or coos when spoken to or smiled at	
Imitates own sounds and vowel sounds produced by others	
Laughs out loud	
Social/Emotional	
Imitates, maintains, terminates, and avoids interactions	
Reacts differently to variations in adult voices	
Enjoys being held and cuddled at times other than feeding and bedtime	
Coos, gurgles, and squeals when awake	
Smiles in response to a friendly face or voice	
Entertains self for brief periods by playing with fingers, hands, and toes	

FOUR TO EIGHT MONTHS

Physical	Date Observed
Parachute reflex appears toward the end of this stage; swallowing reflex appears	
Uses finger and thumb (pincer grip) to pick up objects	
Reaches for objects with both arms simultaneously; later reaches with one hand	
Transfers objects from one hand to the other; grasps object using palmar grasp	
Handles, shakes, and pounds objects; puts everything in mouth	
Sits alone without support (holds head erect, back straight, arms propped forward for support)	
Cognitive	
Turns toward and locates familiar voices and sounds	
Uses hand, mouth, and eyes in coordination to explore own body, toys, and surroundings	
Imitates actions, such as pat-a-cake, waving bye-bye, and playing peek-a-boo	

(continues on next page)

FOUR TO EIGHT MONTHS (CONTINUED)

Cognitive	Date Observed
Shows fear of falling from high places, such as changing table, stairs	
Looks over side of crib or high chair for objects dropped; delights in repeatedly throwing objects overboard for adult to retrieve	
Bangs objects together playfully; bangs spoon or toy on table	
Language	
Responds appropriately to own name and simple requests, such as "eat," "wave bye-bye"	
Imitates some nonspeech sounds, such as cough, tongue click, lip smacking	
Produces a full range of vowels and some consonants: r, s, z, th, and w	
Responds to variations in the tone of voice of others	
Expresses emotions (pleasure, satisfaction, anger) by making different sounds	
Babbles by repeating same syllable in a series: ba, ba, ba.	
Social/Emotional	
Delights in observing surroundings; continuously watches people and activities	
Begins to develop an awareness of self as a separate individual from others	
Becomes more outgoing and social in nature: smiles, coos, reaches out	
Distinguishes among, and responds differently, to strangers, teachers, parents, siblings	
Responds differently and appropriately to facial expressions: frowns; smiles	
Imitates facial expressions, actions, and sounds	

EIGHT TO TWELVE MONTHS

Physical	Date Observed
Reaches with one hand leading to grasp an offered object or toy	
Manipulates objects, transferring them from one hand to the other	
Explores new objects by poking with one finger	
Uses deliberate pincer grip to pick up small objects, toys, and finger foods	
Stacks objects; also places objects inside one another	
Releases objects by dropping or throwing; cannot intentionally put an object down	
Begins pulling self to a standing position; begins to stand alone	

Cognitive	Date Observed
Watches people, objects, and activities in the immediate environment	
Shows awareness of distant objects (15 to 20 feet away) by pointing at them	
Reaches for toys that are visible but out of reach	
Continues to drop first item when other toys or items are offered	
Recognizes the reversal of an object: cup upside down is still a cup	
Imitates activities: hitting two blocks together, playing pat-a-cake	
Language	
Babbles or jabbers to initiate social interaction; may shout to attract attention	
Shakes head for "no" and may nod for "yes"	
Responds by looking for voice when name is called	
Babbles in sentence-like sequences; followed by jargon (syllables/sounds with language-like inflection)	
Waves "bye-bye"; claps hands when asked	
Says "da-da" and "ma-ma"	
Social/Emotional	
Exhibits a definite fear of strangers; clings to, or hides behind, parent or caregiver ("stranger anxiety"); resists separating from familiar adult ("separation anxiety")	
Enjoys being near, and included in, daily activities of family members and teachers; is becoming more sociable and outgoing	
Enjoys novel experiences and opportunities to examine new objects	
Shows need to be picked up and held by extending arms upward, crying, or clinging to adult's legs	
Begins to exhibit assertiveness by resisting caregiver's requests; may kick, scream, or throw self on the floor	

ONE-YEAR-OLDS

Physical	Date Observed
Crawls skillfully and quickly; gets to feet unaided	
Stands alone with feet spread apart, legs stiffened, and arms extended for support	
Walks unassisted near the end of this period (most children); falls often; not always able to maneuver around furniture or toys	
Uses furniture to lower self to floor; collapses backward into a sitting position or falls forward on hands and then sits	
Releases an object voluntarily	
Enjoys pushing or pulling toys while walking	

(continues on next page)

ONE-YEAR-OLDS (CONTINUED)

Cognitive	Date Observed
Enjoys object-hiding activities: early on, will search same location for a hidden object; later will search in several locations	
Passes toy to other hand when offered a second object ("crossing the midline")	
Manages three to four objects by setting an object aside (on lap or floor) when presented with a new toy	
Puts toys in mouth less often	
Enjoys looking at picture books	
Demonstrates understanding of functional relationships (objects that belong together)	
Language	
Produces considerable "jargon": combines words/sounds into speech-like patterns	
Uses one word to convey an entire thought (holophrastic speech); later, produces two-word phrases to express a complete thought (telegraphic speech)	
Follows simple directions: "Give Daddy the cup"	
Points to familiar persons, animals, and toys when asked	
Identifies three body parts if someone names them: "Show me your nose (toe, ear)"	
Indicates a few desired objects/activities by name: "bye-bye," "cookie"; verbal request is often accompanied by an insistent gesture	
Social/Emotional	
Remains friendly toward others; usually less wary of strangers	
Helps pick up and put away toys	
Plays alone for short periods and does not play cooperatively	
Enjoys being held and read to	
Imitates adult actions in play	
Enjoys adult attention; likes to know that an adult is near; gives hugs and kisses	

TWO-YEAR-OLDS

Physical	Date Observed
Walks with a more erect, heel-to-toe pattern; can maneuver around obstacles in pathway	
Runs with greater confidence; has fewer falls	
Squats for long periods while playing	

Physical	Date Observed
Climbs stairs unassisted (but not with alternating feet)	
Balances on one foot (for a few moments), jumps up and down, but may fall	
Begins to achieve toilet training (depending on physical and neurological development) although accidents should still be expected; will indicate readiness for toilet training	
Cognitive	
Exhibits better coordinated eye–hand movements; can put objects together, take them apart; fit large pegs into pegboard	
Begins to use objects for purposes other than intended (pushes block around as boat)	
Completes classification based on one dimension (separates toy dinosaurs from toy cars)	
Stares for long moments; seems fascinated by, or engrossed in, figuring out a situation	
Attends to self-selected activities for longer periods of time	
Shows discovery of cause and effect: squeezing the cat makes her scratch	
Language	
Enjoys being read to if allowed to point, make relevant noises, turn pages	
Realizes that language is effective for getting others to respond to needs and preferences	
Uses 50 to 300 different words; vocabulary continuously increasing	
Has broken linguistic code; in other words, much of a two-year-old's talk has meaning to him or her	
Understands more language than can communicate verbally; most two-year-olds' receptive language is more developed than their expressive language	
Utters three- and four-word statements; uses conventional word order to form more complete sentences	
Social/Emotional	
Shows empathy and caring	
Continues to use physical aggression if frustrated or angry (more exaggerated in some children); physical aggression lessens as verbal skills improve	
Expresses frustration through temper tantrums; tantrum frequency peaks during this year; cannot be reasoned with while tantrum is in progress	
Finds it difficult to wait or take turns; often impatient	
Enjoys "helping" with household chores; imitates everyday activities	
Orders parents and teachers around; makes demands and expects immediate compliance	

THREE-YEAR-OLDS

Physical	Date Observed
Walks up and down stairs unassisted using alternating feet; may jump from bottom step, landing on both feet	
Balances momentarily on one foot	
Kicks a large ball, catches a large bounced ball with both arms extended	
Feeds self; needs minimal assistance	
Jumps in place	
Pedals a small tricycle or Bigwheel	
Cognitive	
Listens attentively and makes relevant comments during age-appropriate stories, especially those related to home and family events	
Likes to look at books and may pretend to "read" to others or explain pictures	
Enjoys stories with riddles, guessing, and suspense	
Points with fair accuracy to correct pictures when given sound-alike words: keys–cheese; fish–dish; mouse–mouth	
Plays realistically: feeds doll; hooks truck and trailer together	
Places eight to ten pegs in pegboard, or six round and six square blocks in form board	
Language	
Talks about objects, events, and people not present: "Jerry has a pool in his yard"	
Talks about the actions of others: "Daddy's mowing the grass"	
Adds information to what has just been said: "Yeah, and then he grabbed it back"	
Answers simple questions appropriately	
Asks increasing numbers of questions, including location/identity of objects and people	
Uses increased speech forms to keep conversation going: "What did he do next?" "How come she hid?"	
Social/Emotional	
Seems to understand taking turns, but not always willing to do so	
Laughs frequently; is friendly and eager to please	
Has occasional nightmares and fears the dark, monsters, or fire	
Joins in simple games and group activities, sometimes hesitantly	
Talks to self often	
Uses objects symbolically in play: block of wood may be a truck, a ramp, a bat	

FOUR-YEAR-OLDS

Physical	Date Observed
Walks a straight line (tape or chalk line on the floor)	
Hops on one foot	
Pedals and steers a wheeled toy with confidence; avoids obstacles and oncoming "traffic"	
Climbs ladders, trees, playground equipment	
Jumps over objects 5 or 6 inches (12.5 to 15 cm) high; lands with both feet together	
Runs, starts, stops, and moves around obstacles with ease	
Cognitive	
Stacks at least five graduated cubes largest to smallest; builds a pyramid of six blocks	
Indicates if paired words sound the same or different: sheet–feet, ball–wall	
Names 18–20 uppercase letters near the end of this year; may be able to print several and write own name; may recognize some printed words (especially those that have special meaning)	
Some begin to read simple books (alphabet books with few words per page and many pictures)	
Likes stories about how things grow and operate	
Delights in wordplay, creating silly language	
Language	
Uses the prepositions "on," "in," and "under"	
Uses possessives consistently: "hers," "theirs," "baby's"	
Answers "Whose?" "Who?" "Why?" and "How many?"	
Produces elaborate sentence structures	
Uses almost entirely intelligible speech	
Begins to correctly use the past tense of verbs: "Mommy closed the door," "Daddy went to work."	
Social/Emotional	
Is outgoing and friendly; overly enthusiastic at times	
Changes moods rapidly and unpredictably; often throws tantrum over minor frustrations; sulk over being left out	
Holds conversations and shares strong emotions with imaginary playmates or companions; invisible friends are common	
Boasts, exaggerates, and "bends" the truth with made-up stories or claims; tests limits with "bathroom" talk	
Cooperates with others; participates in group activities	
Shows pride in accomplishments; seeks frequent adult approval	

FIVE-YEAR-OLDS

Physical	Date Observed
Walks backward, heel to toe	
Walks unassisted up and down stairs, alternating feet	
Learns to turn somersaults (should be taught the right way in order to avoid injury)	
Touches toes without flexing knees	
Catches a ball thrown from 3 feet away	
Rides a tricycle or wheeled toy with speed and skillful steering; some learn to ride bicycles, usually with training wheels	
Cognitive	
Forms rectangle from two triangular cuts	
Builds steps with set of small blocks	
Understands concept of same shape, same size	
Sorts objects on the basis of two dimensions, such as color and form	
Sorts objects so that all things in the group have a single common feature	
Understands smallest and shortest; places objects in order from shortest to tallest, smallest to largest	
Language	
Has vocabulary of 1,500 words or more	
Tells a familiar story while looking at pictures in a book	
Uses functional definitions: a ball is to bounce; a bed is to sleep in	
Identifies and names four to eight colors	
Recognizes the humor in simple jokes; makes up jokes and riddles	
Produces sentences with five to seven words; much longer sentences are not unusual	
Social/Emotional	
Enjoys friendships; often has one or two special playmates	
Shares toys, takes turns, plays cooperatively (with occasional lapses); is often quite generous	
Participates in play and activities with other children; suggests imaginative and elaborate play ideas	
Is affectionate and caring, especially toward younger or injured children and animals	
Follows directions and carries out assignments usually; generally does what parent or teacher requests	
Continues to need adult comfort and reassurance, but may be less open in seeking and accepting comfort	

SIX-YEAR-OLDS

Physical	Date Observed
Has increased muscle strength; typically boys are stronger than girls of similar size	
Gains greater control over large and fine motor skills; movements are more precise and deliberate although some clumsiness persists	
Enjoys vigorous physical activity: running, jumping, climbing, and throwing	
Moves constantly, even when trying to sit still	
Has increased dexterity, eye–hand coordination, and improved motor functioning, which facilitate learning to ride a bicycle, swim, swing a bat, or kick a ball	
Enjoys art projects: likes to paint, model with clay, "make things," draw and color, work with wood	
Cognitive	
Shows increased attention; works at tasks for longer periods, although concentrated effort is not always consistent	
Understands simple time markers (today, tomorrow, yesterday) or uncomplicated concepts of motion (cars go faster than bicycles)	
Recognizes seasons and major holidays and the activities associated with each	
Enjoys puzzles, counting and sorting activities, paper-and-pencil mazes, and games that involve matching letters and words with pictures	
Recognizes some words by sight; attempts to sound out words (some may read well by this time)	
Identifies familiar coins: pennies, nickels, dimes, quarters	
Language	
Loves to talk, often nonstop; may be described as a chatterbox	
Carries on adult-like conversations; asks many questions	
Learns five to ten new words daily; vocabulary consists of 10,000 to 14,000 words	
Uses appropriate verb tenses, word order, and sentence structure	
Uses language (not tantrums or physical aggression) to express displeasure: "That's mine! Give it back, you dummy."	
Talks self through steps required in simple problem-solving situations (although the "logic" may be unclear to adults)	
Social/Emotional	
Experiences mood swings: "best friends" then "worst enemies;" loving then uncooperative and irritable; especially unpredictable toward mother or primary caregiver	

(continues on next page)

SIX-YEAR-OLDS (CONTINUED)

Social/Emotional	Date Observed
Becomes less dependent on parents as friendship circle expands; still needs closeness and nurturing but has urges to break away and "grow up"	
Needs and seeks adult approval, reassurance, and praise; may complain excessively about minor hurts to gain more attention	
Continues to be egocentric; still sees events almost entirely from own perspective: views everything and everyone as there for child's own benefit	
Easily disappointed and frustrated by self-perceived failure	
Has difficulty composing and soothing self; cannot tolerate being corrected or losing at games; may sulk, cry, refuse to play, or reinvent rules to suit own purposes	

SEVEN-YEAR-OLDS

Physical	Date Observed
Exhibits large and fine motor control that is more finely tuned	
Tends to be cautious in undertaking more challenging physical activities, such as climbing up or jumping down from high places	
Practices a new motor skill repeatedly until mastered then moves on to something else	
Finds floor more comfortable than furniture when reading or watching television; legs often in constant motion	
Uses knife and fork appropriately, but inconsistently	
Tightly grasps pencil near the tip; rests head on forearm, lowers head almost to the table top when doing pencil-and-paper tasks	
Cognitive	
Understands concepts of space and time in both logical and practical ways: a year is "a long time"; 100 miles is "far away"	
Begins to grasp Piaget's concepts of conservation (the shape of a container does not necessarily reflect what it can hold)	
Gains a better understanding of cause and effect: "If I'm late for school again, I'll be in big trouble."	
Tells time by the clock and understands calendar time—days, months, years, seasons	
Plans ahead: "I'm saving this cookie for tonight."	
Shows marked fascination with magic tricks; enjoys putting on "shows" for parents and friends	

Language	Date Observed
Enjoys storytelling; likes to write short stories, tell imaginative tales	
Uses adult-like sentence structure and language in conversation; patterns reflect cultural and geographical differences	
Becomes more precise and elaborate in use of language; greater use of descriptive adjectives and adverbs	
Uses gestures to illustrate conversations	
Criticizes own performance: "I didn't draw that right," "Her picture is better than mine."	
Verbal exaggeration commonplace: "I ate ten hot dogs at the picnic."	
Social/Emotional	
Is cooperative and affectionate toward adults and less frequently annoyed with them; sees humor in everyday happenings	
Likes to be the "teacher's helper"; eager for teacher's attention and approval but less obvious about seeking it	
Seeks out friendships; friends are important, but can stay busy if no one is available	
Quarrels less often, although squabbles and tattling continue in both one-on-one and group play	
Complains that family decisions are unjust, that a particular sibling gets to do more or is given more	
Blames others for own mistakes; makes up alibis for personal shortcomings: "I could have made a better one, but my teacher didn't give me enough time."	

EIGHT-YEAR-OLDS

Physical	Date Observed
Enjoys vigorous activity; likes to dance, roller blade, swim, wrestle, bicycle, fly kites	
Seeks opportunities to participate in team activities and games: soccer, baseball, kickball	
Exhibits significant improvement in agility, balance, speed, and strength	
Copies words and numbers from blackboard with increasing speed and accuracy; has good eye–hand coordination	
Possesses seemingly endless energy	
Cognitive	
Collects objects; organizes and displays items according to more complex systems; bargains and trades with friends to obtain additional pieces	

(continues on next page)

EIGHT-YEAR-OLDS (CONTINUED)

Cognitive	Date Observed
Saves money for small purchases; eagerly develops plans to earn cash for odd jobs; studies catalogues and magazines for items to purchase	
Begins taking an interest in what others think and do; understands there are differences of opinion, cultures, distant countries	
Accepts challenge and responsibility with enthusiasm; delights in being asked to perform tasks at home and in school; interested in being rewarded	
Likes to read and work independently; spends considerable time planning and making lists	
Understands perspective (shadow, distance, shape); drawings reflect more realistic portrayal of objects	
Language	
Delights in telling jokes and riddles	
Understands and carries out multiple-step instructions (up to five steps); may need directions because of not listening to the entire request	
Enjoys writing letters or sending e-mail messages to friends; includes imaginative and detailed descriptions	
Uses language to criticize and compliment others; repeats slang and curse words.	
Understands and follows rules of grammar in conversation and written form	
Is intrigued with learning secret word codes and using code language	
Converses fluently with adults; can think and talk about past and future: "What time are we leaving to get to the swim meet next week?"	
Social/Emotional	
Begins forming opinions about moral values and attitudes; declares things right or wrong	
Plays with two or three "best" friends, most often the same age and gender; also enjoys spending some time alone	
Seems less critical of own performance but is easily frustrated when unable to complete a task or when the product does not meet expectations	
Enjoys team games and activities; values group membership and acceptance by peers	
Continues to blame others or makes up alibis to explain own shortcomings or mistakes	
Enjoys talking on the telephone with friends	

PLAY MATERIALS FOR CHILDREN

(Some ideas adapted from M. Bronson, *The Right Stuff for Children Birth to 8: Selecting Play Materials to Support Development.*Washington, DC: NAEYC, 1995.)

Children construct their own understanding of the world around them as they interact with appropriate materials and with other people. Teachers play an important role in providing choices of good-quality playthings that match children's developmental abilities and interests. When budgets are limited, it is vital for teachers to be able to select toys and materials that will provide optimum learning opportunities. Creative teachers learn how to "scrounge" for toys, and to make playthings out of recycled materials. Families often need guidance in choosing playthings that are appropriate for their children's developmental level.

CRITERIA FOR SELECTING PLAY EQUIPMENT FOR YOUNG CHILDREN

A young child's playthings should be as free of detail as possible.

- Too much detail hampers a child's freedom to express himself.

- "Unstructured" toys, which allow the imagination free rein, include blocks, construction sets, clay, sand, and paints.

A good plaything should stimulate children to do things for themselves.

- Equipment that makes the child a spectator may entertain but has little or no play value.

- Play equipment is appropriate when it encourages children to explore and create or offer dramatic play potential.

Young children need large, easily manipulated playthings.

- Toys too small can be frustrating because the child's undeveloped muscular coordination cannot handle smaller forms and shapes.

- A child's muscles develop through play so equipment is appropriate when it allows for climbing and balancing, and other gross motor activity.

The material of which a plaything is constructed has an important role in the play of the young child, and should be considered.

- Warmth and pleasurable touch are significant (wood and cloth have been established as the most satisfactory materials).

- The plaything's durability is of utmost importance.

- Play materials must be sturdy; axles and wheels must be able to support a child's weight.

- Children hate to see their toys break.

- Some materials break readily, proving them to be expensive.

The toy must "work."

- Be sure parts move correctly and that maintenance will be easy.

A plaything's construction should be simple enough for a child to comprehend.

- This strengthens his understanding and experience of the world around him.

- Mechanics should be visible and easily grasped; small children will take them apart to see how they tick.

A plaything should encourage cooperative play.

- Provide an environment that stimulates children to work and play together.

The total usefulness of the plaything must be considered in comparing price.

■ Will it last several children through several stages of their playing lives?

The lists that follow suggest the materials that are priorities for children at particular levels of development.

FOR YOUNG INFANTS (BIRTH THROUGH SIX MONTHS)

■ unbreakable mirrors that can be attached low on walls, or near changing tables and cribs

■ stuffed toys or rag dolls, with stitched faces and eyes, and washable

■ mobiles and visuals hung out of reach

■ grasping toys: simple rattles, squeeze toys, keys on ring, clutch or texture balls

■ hanging toys for batting

■ wrist or ankle bells

FOR OLDER, MOBILE INFANTS (SEVEN THROUGH TWELVE MONTHS)

■ soft rubber animals for grasping

■ simple one-piece vehicles 6–8 inches, with large wheels

■ grasping toys for skill development: toys on suction cups, stacking rings, nesting cups, squeeze toys, plastic pop beads, bean bags, busy boxes

■ containers and objects to fill and dump

■ small cloth, plastic, and board books

■ soft cloth or foam blocks for stacking

■ simple floating objects for water play

■ balls of all kinds, including some with special effects

■ low soft climbing platforms

■ large unbreakable mirrors

■ infant swings for outdoors

■ recorded music and songs

FOR TODDLERS (ONE TO THREE YEARS)

For Fine Motor Skills

- nesting materials
- sand and water play toys: funnels, colanders, small sand tools
- simple activity boxes, with doors, lids, switches, more complex after about 18 months: turning knob or key
- pegboards with large pegs
- 4- to 5-piece stacking materials
- pop beads and stringing beads
- simple 3- to 5-piece puzzles, with knobs, familiar shapes
- simple matching materials
- books, including tactile books, cloth, plastic, and board picture books

For Gross Motor Skills

- push-and-pull toys
- simple doll carriages and wagons
- stable riding toys with four wheels and no pedals
- balls of all sizes
- tunnels for crawling through
- tumbling mats and low climbing platforms

For Pretend Play

- small wood or plastic people and animal figures
- small cars and trucks
- dolls
- plastic dishes and pots and pans
- doll beds
- hats
- simple dress-ups

- telephones
- scarves and fabrics

For Sensory Play

- recorded music and player
- play dough
- fingerpaint
- large nontoxic crayons
- sturdy paper
- simple musical instruments

FOR CHILDREN AGES THREE THROUGH FIVE

For Gross Motor Play

- small wagons and wheelbarrows
- replications of adult tools for pushing and pretend play, such as lawn mower, shopping cart
- scooters
- tricycles and other vehicles with steering ability
- riding toys for more than one child
- balls of all sizes, especially 10–12-inch balls for kicking and throwing
- hollow plastic bat and lightweight ball
- jump rope
- stationary outdoor climbing equipment
- slides and ladders
- outdoor building materials, tires, and other loose parts

Exploration and Mastery Play Materials

- sand and water play: measures, funnels, tubes, sand tools
- construction materials: unit blocks, large hollow blocks
- Lego-type plastic interlocking blocks

- puzzles, including fit-in puzzles and large, simple jigsaw puzzles, with varying numbers of pieces, according to children's age

- pattern-making materials: beads for stringing, pegboards, mosaic boards, feltboards, color cubes

- dressing, lacing, and stringing: sewing cards and dressing frames

- collections of small plastic objects for matching, sorting, and ordering, by color, shape, size, or other category concepts

- simple, concrete number materials for counting and matching to numerals

- measuring materials: scales, measuring cups for liquids

- science materials: magnifying glass, color paddles, objects from the natural world, including pets

- beginning computer programs

- games: dominoes, lotto games, bingo by color, number, or picture, first board games that use concepts such as color or counting, memory

- books of all kinds: picture books, realistic stories, alphabet picture books, poetry, information books

- writing center materials: clipboards, colored pencils, old calendars, envelopes, notepads, stationery, rubber stamps and ink pads, rulers, magnetic letters, stencil shapes, stickers, file cards and office materials

For Pretend Play

- dolls of various ethnic and gender appearance, with clothes and other accessories and furniture

- housekeeping equipment

- variety of dress-ups, including those related to various roles and themes

- transportation toys

- hand puppets

- animal and human figures for play scenes

- full length, unbreakable mirror

For Creative Play

- art and craft materials: crayons, markers, easel, paintbrushes, paint and fingerpaint, varieties of paper, chalkboard and chalk, safety scissors, glue, collage materials, clay and play dough, and tools to use with them

- workbench with hammer, saw, and nails

- musical instruments

- recorded music for singing, movement and dancing, listening, and for using with rhythm instruments

FOR CHILDREN SIX THROUGH EIGHT YEARS

For Gross Motor Play

- balls and sports equipment for beginning team play, such as soccer, baseball

- complex climbing structures: ropes, ladders, rings, hanging bars

- materials for target practice

- mats for acrobatics

- bicycles and scooters

For Exploration and Mastery Play

- construction materials for large constructions and for creating models, including metal parts and nuts and bolts

- puzzles: 100-piece jigsaw puzzles, three-dimensional puzzles like Rubik's cubes

- craft materials for braiding, weaving, knitting, leather craft, jewelry making, sewing

- pattern-making materials: mosaic tiles, geometric puzzles

- games: word games, simple card games, reading and spelling games, number and counting games, beginning strategy games such as checkers

- materials for specific learning: printing materials, math manipulatives, measuring materials, science materials, and computer programs for language arts, number and concept development, and for problem-solving activities

- books at a variety of levels for beginning readers—see the Resources list in the supplement

For Creative Activities

- variety of markers, colored pencils, chalks, paintbrushes and paints, art papers for tracing and drawing

- clay and tools, including pottery wheel

- workbench with wood and variety of tools

- real instruments such as guitars and recorders

- music for singing and movement

- audiovisual materials for independent use

Remember that recycled materials and other loose parts have many uses for exploration and creativity. These materials can be valuable tools in a number of curriculum areas:

- empty plastic containers—detergent bottles, bleach bottles, old refrigerator containers, which can be used for constructing scoops, storing art materials, and so on

- buttons—all colors and sizes, which are excellent for collages, assemblages, as well as sorting, counting, matching, and so on

- egg shells, which can be washed, dried, and colored with food coloring for art projects

- coffee or shortening cans and lids, which can be covered with adhesive paper and used for storage of art supplies, games, and manipulative materials

- magazines with colorful pictures, which are excellent for making collages, murals, and posters

- scraps of fabric—felt, silk, cotton, oil cloth, and so on, which can be used to make "fabric boards" with the name of each fabric written under a small swatch attached to the board, as well as for collages, puppets, and so on

- yarn scraps, which can be used for separating buttons into sets; also for art activities

- styrofoam scraps

- scraps of lace, bric-a-brac, or decorative trim

- bottles with sprinkler tops, which are excellent for water play and for mixing water as children fingerpaint

- wallpaper books of discontinued patterns

- paper doilies

- discarded wrapping paper

- paint color cards from paint/hardware stores

- old paintbrushes

- old jewelry and beads

- old muffin tins, which are effective for sorting small objects and mixing paint

- tongue depressors or ice cream sticks, which can be use as counters for math, and are good for art construction projects, stick puppets, and so on

- wooden clothespins, which can be used for making "people," for construction projects, for hanging up paintings to dry

(Adapted from Mayesky, M., *Creative Activities for Young Children,* 7 edition, published by Cengage Learning.)

If you are responsible for ordering supplies for your classroom or early childhood program, the following guidelines will be useful.

BASIC PROGRAM EQUIPMENT AND MATERIALS FOR AN EARLY CHILDHOOD CENTER

Indoor Equipment

The early childhood room should be arranged into well-planned areas of interest, such as the housekeeping and doll corner, block building, and so on to encourage children to play in small groups throughout the playroom, engaging in activities of their special interest, rather than attempting to play in one large group.

The early childhood center must provide selections of indoor play equipment from many areas of interest. Selection should be of sufficient quantities so that children can participate in a wide range of activities. Many pieces of equipment can be homemade. Consider the age and developmental levels of the children when making selections.

Playroom Furnishings

- Tables—seat four to six children (18 inches high for three-year-olds, 20–22 inches high for four- and five-year-olds)

- Chairs—10 inches high for three-year-olds, 12–14 inches high for four- and five-year-olds

- Open shelves—26 inches high, 12 inches deep, 12 inches between shelves

- Lockers—12 inches wide, 12 inches deep, 32–36 inches high

Housekeeping or Doll Corner

Item	Number Recommended for 10 Children
Dolls	3
Doll clothes	Variety
Doll bed—should be large enough for a child to get into, bedding	1
Doll high chair	1
Small table, four chairs	1 set
Tea party dishes	6-piece set with tray
Stove—child size, approximately 24 in. high, 23 in. long, 12 in. wide	1
Sink—child size, approximately 24 in. high, 23 in. long, 12 in. wide	1
Refrigerator—child size, approximately 28 in. high, 23 in. long, 12 in. wide	1
Pots and pans, empty food cartons, measuring cups, spoons, and so on	Variety
Mop, broom, dustpan	1
Ironing board and iron	1
Clothespins and clothesline	1
Toy telephones	2
Dress-up box—men's and women's hats, neckties, pocketbooks, shoes, old dresses, scarves, jewelry, and so on	Variety
Mirror	1

Art Supplies

Item	Number Recommended for 10 Children
Newsprint paper (18 × 24 in.)	1 ream
Colored paper—variety	3 packages
Large crayons	10 boxes
Tempera paint—red, yellow, blue, black, white	1 can each
Long-handled paintbrushes—making a stroke from ½ in. to 1 in. wide	10–12
Easels	1
Fingerpaint paper — glazed paper such as shelf, freezer, or butcher's paper	1 roll
Paste	1 quart
Blunt scissors	10
Collage—collection of bits of colored paper, cut-up gift wrappings, ribbons, cotton, string, scraps of fabric, and so on, for pasting	Variety
Magazines for cutting and pasting	Variety
Clay—play dough, homemade dough clay	50 pounds
Cookie cutters, rolling pins	Variety
Smocks or aprons to protect children's clothes	10

Block Building Area

Item	Number Recommended for 10 Children
Unit blocks—purchased or homemade (directions are available)	276 pieces, 11 shapes
Large, lightweight blocks	Variety
Small wooden or rubber animals and people	Variety
Small trucks, airplanes, cars, and boats	12
Medium airplanes	3
Medium boats	2
Medium-sized trucks—12 to 24 in.	3

Music Corner

- record player, tape player, CD player

- suitable records, tapes, and CDs

- rhythm instruments

- dress-up scarves for dancing

Manipulative Toys

Item	Number Recommended for 10 Children
Wooden inlay puzzles—approximately five to twenty pieces	6
Color cone	1
Nested blocks	1
Pegboards—variety of shapes and sizes	1
Large spools and beads for stringing	2 sets
Toys that have parts that fit into one another	2
Lotto games	2
Dominoes	1

Books and Stories (20–30 Books)

A carefully selected book collection for the various age levels should include the following:

- transportation, birds and animals, family life
- community helpers, science, nonsense rhymes
- Mother Goose rhymes, poems, and stories
- homemade picture books
- collection of pictures classified by subject
- library books to enrich the collection

Nature Study and Science

- aquarium or fish bowls
- plastic materials
- magnifying glass, prism, magnet, thermometers
- growing indoor plants, garden plot
- additional material such as stones, leaves, acorns, birds' nests, caterpillars, worms, tadpoles, and so on

Woodworking Center

Basic woodworking operations are

- sanding

- gluing

- hammering

- holding (with a vise or clamp)

- fastening (with screws)

- drilling

- sawing

Materials for a woodworking center include:

- sturdy workbench (or table)

- woodworking tools: broad-headed nails 3/4 inch to 1 1/2 inch long, C-clamp or vise (to hold wood), flat-headed hammer weighing about 12 ounces for beginning woodworking experiences, later a claw hammer may be added, 14 inch saw with ten teeth to the inch

- soft white pine lumber scraps (it is difficult to drive nails into hardwood; plywood is not suitable either); packing boxes of soft pine can be disassembled and used for hammering work

Sand Play

- For outdoors, sand should be confined so it is not scattered over the rest of the playground.

- Outdoor area should be large enough for several children to move about without crowding each other.

- Ledge of 10 to 12 inches around a sandbox can serve as a boundary and provide children with a working surface or a seat.

- Keep sand to 6 to 8 inches below the top of the ledge so that it is less likely to spill out.

- Sand should be about 18 inches deep so children can dig or make tunnels.

- Four or five inches of gravel on the bottom of the sandbox provide drainage.

- Basic equipment: plastic or metal kitchen utensils—cups, spoons, pails, shovels, sifters, funnels, scoops, bowls

Water Play

- Can be either indoor or outdoor activity, depending on climate

- Can use clear plastic water basins on a stand with wheels to allow them to be moved to any area of a room

- When using plastic basins, children can see through the sides and the bottom

- For tables on a carpeted floor, use a plastic runner to protect the carpet

- Materials: Clear tubing, sponges, strainers, funnels, corks, pitchers, and measuring cups; for added interest: rotary beaters, spoons, small bowls, plastic basters, and straws

Outdoor Equipment

Outdoor play equipment should be grouped according to use. For example, plan for both active and quiet play; allow for free areas for use of wheel toys. Suggested basic outdoor play equipment for the early childhood program includes:

- climbing structure(s)

- large and small packing boxes

- slide

- swings with canvas seats

- wagons and wheelbarrows

- pedal toys—tricycles, cars, and so on

- sandbox with spoons, shovels, pails, and so on

- balls

- a variety of salvage materials: rubber tires, tire tubes, lengths of garden hose, ropes, and cardboard boxes

  Note: many activities, such as housekeeping play and art activities, at times can be transferred to the outdoor area.

Use this checklist to evaluate your playground setup:

☐ Pathways are clear and spacious enough between areas so that traffic flows well and equipment does not obstruct the children's movement.

☐ Space and equipment are organized so that children are readily visible and easily supervised by adults.

☐ Different activity areas are separated. (Tricycle paths are separate from swings, sandbox is separate from climbing area.)

☐ Open space is available for active play.

☐ There is some space for quiet play.

☐ Dramatic play can be set up outdoors, as space is available.

☐ Art activities can be set up outdoors.

☐ A portion of the play area is covered for use in wet weather.

☐ A storage area is available for play equipment.

☐ A drinking fountain is available.

☐ The area has readily accessible restrooms.

COMMUNICATING WITH FAMILIES ABOUT PLAY

Many families are unfamiliar with play as the basis for developmentally appropriate early childhood classrooms. They may express concerns about preparing for school when they observe the materials and activities in the classroom. It is important that teachers be prepared to help parents understand how young children learn, and the developmental learning that is embedded in play. Regular communication about this subject, pointing out children's progress and learning in all developmental domains, is an important teacher responsibility. Parents come to understand the active curriculum of play when teachers:

■ Post pictures and description of children's engagement in play, highlighting the areas of learning.

■ Invite parents into the classroom, so they can see the teacher's plan and facilitation of learning.

■ Send newsletters that describe children's specific learning through play.

- Share articles that help explain how play lays foundations for later learning.

- Plan workshops and meetings where parents can view videos or have play experiences to better understand the learning process.

- Maintain portfolios that document children's development and learning progress through work samples, photos, and anecdotal records.

- Take every opportunity to discuss children's play as positive learning experiences.

OBSERVATION AND ASSESSMENT

There are a variety of tools that can be used to assess children's development. Using assessment tools in conjunction with developmental milestones helps caregivers recognize a child's developmental accomplishments as well as determine the child's next growth steps. Not all children will be developing at the same rate, in the same way. The teacher needs to observe each child to determine the level to which each child is performing independently so that instruction can begin. This knowledge is useful in planning curriculum, designing the room environment for success, in establishing appropriate guidance techniques that help children manage their own behavior, and in communicating specific information about each child during parent conferences. No doubt your college practicum experience taught you the logistics of observing: using objective descriptions and recording specific, dated, brief, and factual information. Observation can take many forms:

- anecdotal records

- running records

- checklists

- time or event sampling

ANECDOTAL RECORD

Anecdotal records are brief notes kept by the teacher while the child is performing a task. At first this may seem daunting, but it will become part of your everyday routine. Keep a small spiral notebook and pen or pencil in your pocket. When a child begins an activity, watch what the child does and write down three or four things that you actually observe the child doing. Remember the facts and only the facts. For example:

Johnny stacking unit blocks four high. Another stack of four. Talk about dad, and being architect

As time permits, probably during nap or planning time, the brief notes are turned into a full scenario so that anyone could read the record at a later date:

ANECDOTAL RECORD				
Child's Name: Johnny H.		Age: 7 yr. 5 mo.		
Observer's Name: Jorge		Date: April 27, 2005		

What actually happened/ What I saw	Developmental Interpretation (Select 1 or 2 of the following)			
Johnny was building alone in the clock corner. He stacked four blocks carefully, then made another stack of four beside it. He said, "You have to make the walls exactly even to build a good house. My dad is a builder. I'm going to be an architect." He smiled.	Interest in learning	X	Self-esteem/self-concept	X
	Cultural acceptance		Problem solving	
	Interest in real-life mathematical concepts	X	Interactions with adults	
	Literacy		Interactions with peers	
	Language expression/ comprehension	X	Self-regulation	
	Safe/healthy behavior		Self-help skills	
	Gross motor skills	X	Fine motor skills	

ANECDOTAL RECORD				
Child's Name: _____		Age: _____		
Observer's Name: _____		Date: _____		

What actually happened/ What I saw	Developmental Interpretation (Select 1 or 2 of the following)			
	Interest in learning		Self-esteem/self-concept	
	Cultural acceptance		Problem solving	
	Interest in real-life mathematical concepts		Interactions with adults	
	Literacy		Interactions with peers	
	Language expression/ comprehension		Self-regulation	
	Safe/healthy behavior		Self-help skills	
	Gross motor skills		Fine motor skills	

RUNNING RECORD

Another form of authentic assessment is the running record. It covers a longer time span and gives more information than an anecdotal record. Often it may have a specific developmental focus such as "social interactions." A running record will give you information about other developmental areas because of its very detailed nature. This form of observation requires the caregiver to not be involved with children for several minutes while writing the observation. You will be setting yourself apart from the children and writing continuously, in as much detail as possible. You will write what the child does and says, by herself and in interactions with other people and materials. Use objective phrases and avoid interpretative and judgmental language. Note that the format for this form of assessment has two columns. The left column is for writing the actual observations and the right column is for connecting the observations to aspects of development. Remember to date all observations so you can notice developmental change over time.

RUNNING RECORD

Child's Name: Trish H. Age: 7 yr. 5 mo.

Observer's Name: Jorge Date: April 27, 2005

Developmental Focus: Social interactions with peers

Trish is sitting at the writing table working on her journal. She responds when Michelle asks to borrow her red marker, passing it over. She continues to write, asking Michelle how to spell "birthday." Michelle asks her what she is writing, and Trish responds that she is writing about her grandma's birthday, since she couldn't go visit her for her birthday. Michelle then grabs Trish's blue marker. Trish says, "You need to ask me if you can use that. It's mine. I'll let you use it, but you shouldn't just grab it." Michelle returns it, and the two girls work for five more minutes.	Participates in cooperative activities
	Early literacy/ expressive language
	Expresses empathy
	Communicates knowledge of growing skills
	Self-regulation/ controls emotions
Then they go to join the group who are exercising to music. She stretches her arms high, then twirls on one foot. She says to Michelle, "Count while I see how long I can turn. I bet I can do it for ten seconds, maybe longer." She twirls while Michelle counts, then suggests Michelle turn and she will count. Then she says, "I'm good at balancing because I have learned to ride my bike."	Stands up for own rights
	Asks for what she needs
	Gross motor skills
	Math skill
	Self-awareness

CHECKLIST

A checklist is often used as a means of assessment because it is one of the easiest assessment tools to use. A checklist consists of a pre-determined list of clearly observable developmental criteria for which the observer indicates "yes" or "no." The observer reads the developmental criteria and makes a checkmark if the decision is a "yes." This form of assessment requires that no additional notes be recorded. Many teachers design their own checklists to fit the specific needs of their program. The following checklist is an example of one that might be used to assess social skills of children.

SOCIAL SKILLS CHECKLIST	
Child's Name: _____ Age: _____ yr. _____ mo. Observer's Name: _____	
Skills	**Dates**
☐ Desires and can work near other children	
☐ Interacts with other children	
☐ Takes turns with other children	
☐ Enters play with others in positive manner	
☐ Shares materials and supplies	
☐ Stands up for own rights in positive manner	
☐ Forms friendships with peers	
☐ Engages in positive commentary on other children's work	
☐ Shows empathy	
☐ Negotiates compromises with other children	
☐ Demonstrates pro-social behavior	
☐ Participates in cooperative group activities	
☐ Resolves conflicts with adult prompts	
☐ Resolves conflicts without adult prompts	

Make checklists for each center in your classroom and hang them on clipboards. When you observe the children at play in each center, check off skills by placing a date in the appropriate box.

The last type of observation that a teacher should perform is a time or event sampling. These are similar in focus, but different, too. A time sampling asks the teacher to set a timer and each time the timer goes off, the teacher looks at a particular child and writes down what the child is doing. Again only the facts are written:

The timer is set to go off every ten minutes. I will look at Johnny and see what he is doing when I hear the timer. The timer goes off, I look at Johnny. He is drawing a picture with markers at the art table. The timer goes off again. He has moved to the puzzle table and is working on a puzzle with Roberto.

As mentioned, an event sampling is similar, only the teacher looks at events instead of being directed by a timer. The teacher zeros in on an event and writes down all things that she sees pertaining to the event.

EVENT SAMPLE

Antecedent	Behavior	Consequence
Four children come to the play dough table, with only three places available	Roberto begins to shout that he was here first, and he wants a turn. Sam, Sarah, and Alex ignore him and begin to roll the play dough.	Roberto stands and watches for a few minutes, then goes off to the block area. The other three continue to roll and sculpt play dough for 15 minutes.

All of these observations yield specifics about children and their developmental progress and ways of behaving. Observing over a period of time helps teachers see patterns and trends that are appropriate to share with parents.

Assessment and observation may seem overwhelming as you begin your career in Early Childhood. Do not shy away from it. Take the challenge and begin to look for the positive aspects of learning and mastering a new skill. Picture yourself as a student in your classroom and imagine what it is like to perfect something your teacher has just asked you to do. How does it make you feel? Now begin.

Teachers, no matter whether they work with babies, preschoolers, or school-aged children, are involved in a cycle of planning to create developmentally appropriate learning experiences. That cycle begins and ends with observation, and observation occurs as well throughout the cycle.

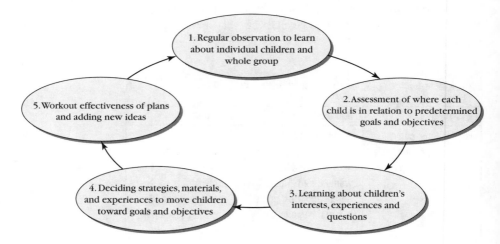

1. Regular observation to learn about individual children and whole group

2. Assessment of where each child is in relation to predetermined goals and objectives

3. Learning about children's interests, experiences and questions

4. Deciding strategies, materials, and experiences to move children toward goals and objectives

5. Workout effectiveness of plans and adding new ideas

In addition, teachers use their observations to assess children's development in relation to specific goals set by the program or school. They also use their knowledge of individual children's interests and experiences to create meaningful learning experiences that will support progress toward those goals. The cycle continues as teachers continue to observe to see how well their plans have succeeded, and make needed modifications. Planning curriculum is purposeful, and specific to the particular group and individuals within the group.

But in addition to this cycle of careful planning, teachers also have to be prepared for the unexpected.

- You have the day planned for outdoor activities and there is an unexpected rainstorm. What will you do?

- It is your day off and you get a call at the last minute to cover for a coworker who is ill. You find out that nothing has been planned. What activities can you implement quickly?

- You were promised that the materials you needed for your planned art activity would be on site when you arrived at work, but there was a shipping delay and they aren't there. What is an alternative activity you can easily set up and implement?

Being prepared at all times with a few back-up activities will make your job much less stressful. Some of the activities listed here require only a few materials that you might want to have on hand at all times. When teachers have supplies of open-ended materials, children can find endless possibilities that match their developmental level.

- tapes or CDs for creative movement indoors, with scarves and streamers for props

- rhythm instruments to play along with the tapes to have a parade

- an obstacle course, created by moving furniture, allowing children to maneuver under tables, around shelves, over chairs, and so on

- a collection of Nerf balls and a target or container, to allow children to practice throwing skills indoors

- water, dishpans or water table, and appropriate utensils for sensory exploration or measuring

- scraps of fabric, paper scraps, and other recycled materials for gluing collage or making small puppets

- boxes, paper towel rolls, glue, and paint for box construction

- flour, salt, and other materials for making an easy play dough recipe with children's assistance

- large sheets of butcher paper for children to make life-sized self-portraits, tracing around each other with markers, filling in their clothing and hair, and then posting up to measure height

- puzzles and other manipulatives that have been stored elsewhere, and are not part of the materials used every day

- a collection of containers and lids of various sizes for matching

- a collection of buttons of various shapes and colors, and muffin tins for sorting and classifying, and doing math games

- a number of large cardboard cartons saved in the closet for use as houses, vehicles, or tunnels (Children can paint them to suit the purpose.)

- the ingredients and a recipe for making individual muffins for snack

- a book of silly poems that you have been saving for a treat

A number of Web sites offer sample lesson plans for teachers. When downloading lesson plans from the Internet or another source, be sure each plan includes

- objective or goal of the lesson

- materials needed

- directions for the activity

- appropriate age group

- developmental appropriateness

Check the resources section of this manual for a list of Web sites with lesson plans and other free materials for teachers.

BOOKS FOR CHILDREN

Reading aloud is a wonderful gift you can give to children. Through sharing an interesting book, you introduce them to a world they might not otherwise be able to visit. You can travel anywhere you like; you can have experiences that are outside the realm of your current environment; you can participate in wonderful fantasies; you can be saddened, then uplifted.

Children's desire to read and the ability to do so is fostered by being read to as soon as they are born. Even babies can enjoy looking at picture books and hearing simple stories. Preschoolers love to have favorite books read to them repeatedly. As children move into the school years, they can sustain their interest in longer books that are divided into chapters. When they realize the joy that comes from good books, they are more motivated to read on their own.

Many textbooks provide suggestions for setting up reading corners and providing books for children to read by themselves. This section will focus on books that you can read aloud to children in small or large groups. Remember that the more you read, the better you will become at doing so. When the books have been enjoyed in a group setting, add them to the book corner for children to read alone. In addition, teachers often create lending arrangements where children can take home books for their parents to read and then return. Teachers who believe in the importance of reading choose the best of children's literature and involve families in reading.

HOW TO GET CHILDREN TO LISTEN AND WANT MORE

- Read to children regularly, individually and in groups. Schedule time each day for reading, maybe toward the end of the day when children are tired and will enjoy the inactivity; make sure the setting is comfortable.

- Choose books that you also enjoy, perhaps one you read as a child, or those you find on lists of good books for children. Preview the book before presenting it to the children. You may find passages that you will want to shorten.

- The first time you read a book, state the title and author. Research for interesting facts about the author to share with the children. If there is an illustrator, include that information as well.

- If you are reading to a large group, position yourself so that you are slightly higher than the children so that your voice will project more easily.

- If you are reading to a small group, sit among them in a more intimate placement, which will draw them to you and the book.

- Occasionally stop and ask, "What do you think is going to happen next?"

- Read at a pace that allows children to build mental images of the characters or setting; change your pace to match the action of the story: slow your pace and lower your voice during a suspenseful spot and then speed up when the action does.

- Allow time for discussion only if children wish to do so. Let them voice fears, ask questions, or share their thoughts about the book. Do not turn it into a quiz or need to interpret the story.

- Practice reading aloud, trying to vary your expression or tone of voice.

- If you are reading a chapter book to older children, create a display of images or information pertaining to the book you are reading. A map will allow children to pinpoint places mentioned in the story. Pictures, charts, or time lines will also add to the display. Objects or foods mentioned in the book add another dimension.

- Again, with chapter books for older children, find a stopping place each day that will create suspense, so that the children are eager to get back to the book the next day.

- When you pick up the book the next day, ask if they remember what had happened just before you stopped reading.

- Encourage families to read regularly to their children, by providing books on loan, booklists, and information on the importance of reading to foster literacy development.

WHAT NOT TO DO

- Don't read a book you do not enjoy; your feelings will be sensed by the children.

- Don't read a book when it becomes obvious that it was a poor choice; previewing the book before presenting it to the children can minimize these kinds of mistakes.

- Don't always choose a book with which some of the children are already familiar; they may have heard it at home or seen a version on television or the movies.

- Don't start a book unless you have enough time to read more than a few pages.

- Don't be fooled by awards. Just because a book has received a national book award does not mean that it is suitable for your particular group of children.

- Don't impose on the children your own interpretations or reactions to the story on the children, or quiz them to see what they got out of it. Let them express their own understanding and feelings.

It is important to use good children's literature to convey acceptance of the many family forms in today's world, as well as the particular circumstances of families. The following lists may be particularly useful.

BOOKS ABOUT ALL KINDS OF FAMILIES

Ackerman, K. (1999). *By the Dawn's Early Light*. Aladdin. (Mom works the night shift)

Adoff, A. (2004). *Black Is Brown Is Tan*. Amistad. (interracial family)

Aylette, J. (1993). *Families: A Celebration of Diversity, Commitment, and Love.* Houghton Mifflin. (photos and descriptions of all kinds of families)

Bauer, C. (1985). *My Mom Travels a Lot.* Puffin Books.

Baum, L. (1986). *One More Time.* Morrow. (child going between mom's house and dad's house)

Blain, M. (1983). *The Terrible Thing that Happened at Our House.* Scholastic. (Mom starts work)

Blomquist, G., & Blomquist, F. (1991). *Zachary's New Home: A Story for Foster and Adopted Children.* Magination Press.

Bosch, S. (1983). *Jenny Lives with Eric and Martin.* Gay Men's Press. (two fathers)

Boyd, L. (1992). *Sam Is My Half-Brother.* Puffin Books.

Bunting, E. (1993). *Fly Away Home.* Clarion Books. (homeless child and father)

————. (2000). *Can You Do This, Old Badger?* Harcourt Children's Books. (living with grandparent)

Cowen-Fletcher, J. (1996). *Mama Zooms.* Scholastic. (mother in a wheelchair)

Crews, D. (1998). *Bigmama's.* HarperTrophy. (extended family)

Drescher, J. (1980). *Your Family, My Family.* Walker. (different shapes and sizes)

Eichler, M. (1977). *Martin's Father.* Lollipop Power. (nurturing single father)

Eisenberg, P. (1995). *You're My Nikki.* Puffin Books. (new working mother)

Falwell, C. (1995). *Feast for 10.* Clarion Books. (large family)

Galloway, P. (1980). *Good Times, Bad Times—Mummy and Me.* Women's Press. (working single mother)

————. (1983). *Jennifer Has Two Daddies.* Women's Press. (child alternates weeks with her mom and stepdad and her father)

Hayes, M., & Witherell, J. (1989). *My Daddy Is in Prison.* Head Start.

Hickman, M. (1995). *Robert Lives with his Grandparents.* Albert Whitman & Co.

Hines, A. (1999). *Daddy Makes the Best Spaghetti.* Clarion Books.

Jenness, A. (1993). *Families.* Houghton Mifflin.

Kapp, A. (1979). *All Kinds of Mothers.* Deseret Books. (mothers who work both in and out of home)

Kroll, V. (1995). *Wood-Hoopoe Willie.* Charlesbridge Publ. (African American family)

Kuklin, S. (1998). *How My Family Lives in America.* Aladdin. (real stories of different ethnic backgrounds)

Lasker, J. (1972). *Mothers Can Do Anything.* Albert Whitman & Co. (many jobs mothers do)

Loewen, I. (1986). *My Mom Is so Unusual.* Pemmican Pubs. (contemporary American Indian)

Maslac, H. (1996). *Finding a Job for Daddy.* Albert Whitman. (unemployed father)

Merriam, E. (1996). *Mommies at Work.* Little Simon. (in and out of home work)

Moore, E. (1985). *Grandma's House.* Lothrop, Lee, and Shepherd. (spending the summer with an active, nontraditional grandmother)

Newman, L. (1991). *Gloria Goes to Gay Pride.* Alyson Pub.

Pelligrini, N. (1991). *Families Are Different.* Holiday House.

Quinlan, P. (1987). *My Dad Takes Care of Me.* Annick Press. (unemployed father at home)

Rotner, S., & Kelly, S. (1996). *Lots of Moms.* Dial.

Schlein, M. (2000). *The Way Mothers Are.* Albert Whitman.

Schwartz, A. (1987). *Oma and Bobo.* Atheneum. (mother, grandmother, and child)

Simon, N. (1976). *All Kinds of Families.* Albert Whitman.

Skutch, R. (1997). *Who's in a Family?* Tricycle Press.

Soto, G. (1996). *Too Many Tamales.* Putnam. (Mexican American family)

Spelman, C. (1996). *After Charlotte's Mom Died.* Albert Whitman. (single father)

Stinson, K. (1984). *Mom and Dad Don't Live Together Any More.* Firefly Books. (divorce)

Wickens, E. (1994). *Anna Day and the O-Ring*. Alyson Pubs. (two mothers)

Valentine, J. (2004). *One Dad, Two Dads, Brown Dad, Blue Dads*. Alyson Pubs.

Vigna, J. (1995). *My Two Uncles*. Albert Whitman.

Wild, M. (1993). *Space Travellers*. Scholastic. (homeless)

Willhoite, M. (1991). *Daddy's Roommate*. Alyson Pubs. (divorced parent, gay father)

Williams, V. (1991). *A Chair for My Mother*. HarperTrophy. (three generations of urban working-class family)

BOOKS ABOUT SEPARATION AND STARTING SCHOOL

Ahlberg, J., & Ahlberg, A. (1990). *Starting School*. Puffin Books.

————. (1997). *Peek-a-Boo!* Viking.

Albee, S. (2001). *I Don't Want to Go to School*. Random House.

Amoss, B. (1972). *The Very Worst Thing*. Parents Magazine Press.

Anholt, L. (2005). *Going to Playgroup*. Orchard Books.

Aseltine, L. (1988). *First Grade Can Wait*. Albert Whitman.

Baker, C. F. (1985). *My Mom Travels a Lot*. Puffin Books.

Barkan, J. (1994). *Anna Marie's Blanket*. Barrons Juveniles.

Barkin, C., & James, E. (1975). *I'd Rather Stay Home*. Heinemann Library.

Berenstain, S., & Berenstain, J. (2005). *The Berenstain Bears Go Back to School*. HarperCollins.

Berger, T. (1974). *A Friend Can Help*. Heinemann Library.

Blue, R. (1971). *I Am Here: Yo Estoy Aqui*. Franklin Watts.

Boelts, M. (1996). *Little Bunny's Preschool Countdown*. Albert Whitman.

Brand, J., & Gladstone, N. (1985). *My Day Care Book*. Acropolis Books.

Bunnett, R. (1995). *Friends at School*. Star Bright Books.

Burningham, J (1976). *The Friend*. Crowell.

.————. (1977). *The Blanket.* HarperCollins.

Civardi, A. (1994). *First Experiences: Going to School.* EDC Pub.

Chalmers, M. (1981). *Be Good Harry.* Trophy Press.

Cohen, M. (1989). *The New Teacher.* Aladdin.

.————. (1989). *See You Tomorrow, Charlie.* Yearling.

.————. (1989). *Will I Have a Friend?* Aladdin.

Coles, M. (1984). *Michael's First Day at School.* Hodder and Stoughton.

Cooney, N. (1981). *The Blanket That Had to Go.* Putnam.

Corey, D. (1999). *You Go Away.* Albert Whitman.

Crary, E. (1996). *Mommy Don't Go.* Parenting Press.

DeGroat, D. (2005). *Brand-new Pencils, Brand-new Books.* Harper-Collins.

Delacre, L. (1989). *Time for School, Nathan!* Scholastic.

Eastman, P. (1960). *Are You My Mother?* Random House.

Elliott, D. (1992). *Grover Goes to School.* Random House.

Harris, R. (2004). *Don't Forget to Come Back.* Candlewick.

Henkes, K. (1993). *Owen.* Greenwillow.

Hill, E. (1984). *Spot Goes to School.* Putnam.

Hines, A. (1986). *Don't Worry, I'll Find You.* Dutton.

Howe, J. (1995). *When You Go to Kindergarten.* HarperTrophy.

Hurwitz, J. (2001). *Rip-Roaring Russell.* HarperTrophy.

Johnson, D. (1990). *What Will Mommy Do When I'm at School?* Atheneum.

Kantrowitz, M. (1989). *Willy Bear.* Aladdin Paperback.

Lionni, L. (1995). *Little Blue and Little Yellow.* HarperTrophy.

Mayer, M. (1980). *Frog, Where Are You?* Puffin.

Molnar, D., and Fenton, S. (1991). *Who Will Pick Me Up When I Fall?* Albert Whitman.

Oh, J. (2005). *Mr. Monkey's Classroom.* HarperCollins.

Park, S. (2003). *Sumi's First Day of School Ever.* Viking Books.

Penn, A. (1993). *The Kissing Hand*. Child and Family Press.

Rogers, F. (1985). *Going to Day Care*. Putnam.

Simon, N. (1980). *I'm Busy Too*. Albert Whitman.

Skarmeas, N. (2001). *My First Day of School*. Candy Cane Press.

Smath, J. (1984). *Elephant Goes to School*. Parents Magazine Press.

Soderstrom, M. (1981). *Maybe Tomorrow I'll Have a Good Time*. Human Sciences Press.

Sperring, M. (2005). *Wanda's First Day*. Gardners Books.

Stiles, N. (2005). *On My Very First School Day I Met...* Milk and Cookies.

Sturges, P. (2004). *I Love School*. HarperCollins.

Tompert, A. (1992). *Will You Come Back for Me?* Albert Whitman.

Warren, C. (1984). *Fred's First Day*. William Morrow and Co.

Wells, R. (2000). *Timothy Goes to School*. Puffin Books.

————. (2004). *My Kindergarten*. Hyperion.

Wild, M. (2000). *Tom Goes to Kindergarten*. Albert Whitman.

Winget, S. (2005). *Tucker's Four-Carrot School Day*. HarperCollins.

Wolde, B. (1992). *Betsy's First Day of Nursery School*. Random House.

BOOKS ABOUT DIVORCE

Ballard, Robin. (1993). *Gracie*. Greenwillow.

Baum, Louis. (1986). *One More Time*. Morrow.

Bienenfeld, F. (1980). *My Mom and Dad Are Getting a Divorce*. EMC Pubs.

Boeltz, J. (2004). *With My Mom, With My Dad*. Zonderkidz.

Brown, Laurene K., & Brown, Marc. (1986). *Dinosaurs Divorce*. Marc Brown.

Caines, J. (1977). *Daddy*. HarperCollins.

Carney, K. (1997). *Together We'll Get Through This*. Dragonfly Pubs.

Forrai, M. (1977). *A Look at Divorce*. Lerner Pub. Group.

Gardner, R. (1985). *The Boys and Girls Book about Divorce*. Bantam.

Girard, Linda. (1991). *At Daddy's on Saturdays*. Albert Whitman.

Goff, Beth. (1985). *Where Is Daddy? The Story of a Divorce*. Beacon Press.

Haughton, E. (2004). *Rainy Day*. Lerner Pub.

Hazen, Barbara. (1983). *Two Homes to Live In: A Child's-Eye View of Divorce*. Human Sciences Press.

Kelly, K. (2004). *Lucy Rose: Here's the thing about Me*. Delacorte Books for Young Readers.

Kimball, G. (1994). *How to Survive your Parents' Divorce: Kids' Advice to Kids*. Equality Press.

Lach, M., Loughridge, S., & Fassler, D. (1990). *My Kind of Family: A Book for Kids in Single-Parent Homes*. Waterfront Books.

Lansky, V. (1998). *It's Not Your Fault KokoBear: A Read-together Book for Parents and Young Children during Divorce*. Book Peddlers.

LeShan, E. (1987). *What's Going to Happen to Me?* Aladdin.

Lindsay, Jeanne Warren. (1999). *Do I Have a Daddy: A Story about a Single-Parent Child*. Morning Glory Press.

MacGregor, C. (2001). *The Divorce Helpbook for Kids*. Impact Pubs.

Masurel, C. (2003). *Two Homes*. Candlewick.

Mayle, P. (1980). *Divorce Can Happen to the Nicest People*. Macmillan.

———. (1988). *Why Are We Getting a Divorce?* Harmony.

McCoy, J. (2003). *Two Old Potatoes and Me*. Knopf.

McGinnis, L. (1995). *If Daddy Only Knew Me*. Albert Whitman.

Nightingale, L. (1996). *My Parents Still Love Me Even Though They're Getting a Divorce: An Interactive Tale for Children*. Nightingale Rose Pubs.

Prestine, J. S. (2001). *Mom and Dad Break Up*. Fearon.

Ransom, J. (2000). *I Don't Want to Talk About It*. Magination Press.

Rodell, S. (1995). *Dear Fred*. Viking.

Rogers, F. (1996). Let's Talk About It: *Divorce*. Putnam.

Sanford, D. (1986). *Please Come Home: A Child's Book about Divorce*. Gold N Honey.

Schindel, J. (1995). *Dear Daddy.* Albert Whitman.

Simon, Norma. (1983). *I Wish I Had My Father.* Albert Whitman.

Spellman, C. (1998). *Mama and Daddy Bear's Divorce.* Albert Whitman.

Stern, Z., & Stern, E. (1997). *Divorce Is Not the End of the World: Zoe's and Evan's Coping Guide for Kids.* Tricycle Press.

Stinson, Kathy. (1984). *Mom and Dad Don't Live Together Any More.* Annick Press.

Thomas, P. (1999). *My Family's Changing.* Barron's.

Vigna, Judith. (1987). *Mommy and Me by Ourselves Again.* Albert Whitman.

Weninger, B. (1997). *Good-bye Daddy!* Michael Neugebauer.

Willner-Pardo, G. (1994). *What I'll Remember When I'm a Grownup.* Clarion.

Winchester, K., et al. (2001). *What in the World Do You Do When Your Parents Divorce? A Survival Guide for Kids.* Sagebrush.

Wyeth, S. (1996). *Ginger Brown: Too Many Houses.* Random House.

BOOKS ABOUT STEPFAMILIES

Ballard, R. (1998). *When I Am a Sister.* Greenwillow.

Bender, E. (1998). *Search for a Fawn.* Herald Press.

Berman, C. (1992). *What Am I Doing in a Stepfamily?* Carol Publ.

Bowdish, L. (1997). *Living with my Stepfather Is Like Living with a Moose.* Farrar, Straus, and Giroux.

Bunting, E. (2000). *The Memory String.* Clarion.

Cook, J. (1995). *Room for a Stepdaddy.* Albert Whitman.

Helmering, D. (1981). *I Have Two Families.* Abingdon.

Herman, G. (2001). *Just Like Mike.* Yearling.

Hoffman, M. (2000). *Boundless Grace: Sequel to Amazing Grace.* Puffin.

Holub, J. (2001). *Cinderdog and the Wicked Stepcat.* Albert Whitman.

Jukes, M. (1987). *Like Jake and Me.* Dragonfly Books.

Marshall, L. (1991). *What Is a Step?* Native Sun Publ.

Monroe, R. (1998). *I Have a New Family Now: Understanding Blended Families*. Concordia Publishing House.

Park, B. (1998). *My Mother Got Married and Other Disasters*. Sagebrush.

Parks, C. (2001). *The Beautiful Duckling*. Providence House Publ.

Rogers. F. (2001). *Let's Talk about It—Stepfamilies*. Putnam.

Schwab, L. (1995). *My Dad Is Getting Married Again*. Center for Applied Psychology.

Seuling, B. (1995). *What Kind of Family Is This? A Book about Stepfamilies*. Golden Books.

Taylor, L. (2000). *My Whole Family*. Changing Lives Pubs.

Venable, L. (1999). *The Not So Wicked Stepmother, a Book for Children and Adults*. L.A. Venable Pubs.

Vigna, J. (1980). *She's Not my Real Mother*. Albert Whitman.

———. (1982). *Daddy's New Baby*. Albert Whitman.

Weitzman, E. (1997). *Let's Talk about Living in a Blended Family*. PowerKids Press.

BOOKS ABOUT ABUSE IN FAMILIES

Bass, E. et al. (1993). *I Like You to Make Jokes with Me, but I don't Want You to Touch Me*. Lollipop Power.

Behm, B. (1999). *Tears of Joy*. Wayword Publ.

Boyd, C., & Cooper, F. (1995). *Daddy, Daddy, Be There*. Philomel Books.

Carrick, C. (1995). *Banana Beer*. Concept Books.

Cavaciuti. (2001). *Someone Hurt Me*. Creativity Publ.

Clifton, L. (2001). *One of the Problems of Everett Anderson*. Henry Holt.

Davis, D. (1984). *Something Is Wrong at My House*. Parenting Press.

DiGiovanni, K. (1986). *My House Is Different*. Hazelden.

Girard, L. (1992). *My Body Is Private*. Albert Whitman.

Havelin, K. (2000). *Child Abuse: Why Do My Parents Hit Me?* Capstone Press.

Hornbum, T. (1994). *Hear My Roar: A Story of Family Violence.* Annick Press.

Katz, I. et al. (1994). *Sarah.* Real Life Story Books.

Kehoe, P. (1987). *Something Happened and I'm Scared to Tell: A Book for Young Victims of Abuse.* Parenting Press.

Kleven, S. (1998). *The Right Touch: A Read Aloud Story to Help Prevent Child Sexual Abuse.* Illumination Arts Press.

McAndrew, L. (1999). *Little Flower: A Story for Children.* CWLA Press.

Otto, M. (1988). *Never, No Matter What.* Women's Press.

Paris, S. (1986). *Mommy and Daddy Are Fighting.* Seal Press.

Porett, J. (1999). *When I Was Little Like You.* CWLA Press.

Sanford, D. (1988). *I Know the World's Worst Secret: A Child's Book about Living with an Alcoholic Parent.* Multnomah Pub.

Spelman, C. (2000). *Your Body Belongs to You.* Albert Whitman.

Stanek, M. (1983). *Don't Hurt Me Mama.* Albert Whitman.

Vigna, J. (1993). *I Wish Daddy Didn't Drink So Much.* Albert Whitman.

———. (1995). *My Big Sister Takes Drugs.* Albert Whitman.

Williams, C. (1998). *The True Colors of Caitlynne Jackson.* Yearling.

Winn, C., & Walsh, D. (1996). *Clover's Secret.* Fairview Press.

BOOKS ABOUT ADOPTION

Banish, R., & Jordan-Wong, J. (1992). *A Forever Family.* HarperCollins.

Bunin, C., & Bunin, S. (1992). *Is That Your Sister?* Our Child Press.

Burwash, L. (1998). *All about Me: Adopted and Special; An Interactive Tool for Parents and Children.* All About Me.

Cole, J. (1999). *How I Was Adopted: Samantha's Story.* HarperTrophy.

Cosby, E. (2000). *A Is for Adopted.* DIR Group.

Curtis, J. L. (1996). *Tell Me Again: About the Night I Was Born.* Joanna Cotter.

D'Antonio, N. (1997). *Our Baby from China: An Adoption Story.* Albert Whitman.

Girard, L. (1991). *Adoption Is for Always.* Albert Whitman.

———. (1992). *We Adopted You, Benjamin Koo.* Albert Whitman.

Kasza, K. (1996). *A Mother for Choco.* Putnam.

Katz, K. (1997). *Over the Moon: An Adoption Tale.* Henry Holt and Co.

Keller, H. (1991). *Horace.* Greenwillow.

Kitze, C. (2003). *We See the Moon.* EMK Press.

———. (2003). *I don't Have Your Eyes.* EMK Press.

Koehler, P. (1997). *The Day We Met You.* Aladdin.

Kroll, V. (1994). *Beginnings: How Families Come to Be.* Albert Whitman.

Lewis, R. (2000). *I Love You Like Crazycakes.* Little, Brown.

Lifton, B. (1994). *Tell Me a Real Adoption Story.* Knopf Books.

Livingston, C. (1997). *Why Was I Adopted?* Lyle Stuart.

London, J. (1997). *A Koala for Katie: An Adoption Story.* Albert Whitman.

McCutcheon, J. (1996). *Happy Adoption Day.* Little, Brown.

Miller, K. (1994). *Did My First Mother Love Me?* Morning Glory Press.

Mora, P. (1994). *Pablo's Tree.* Simon and Schuster.

Nystrom, C. (1987). *Mario's Big Question.* Lion Publ.

Peacock, C. (2000). *Mommy Far, Mommy Near: An Adoption Story.* Albert Whitman.

Rogers, F. (1998). *Let's Talk About It: Adoption.* Paperstar Books.

Rosove, L. (2001). *Rosie's Family: An Adoption Story.* Asia Press.

Schwartz, P. (1996). *Carolyn's Story: A Book about an Adopted Girl.* Lerner Publ. Group.

Sobol, H. (1984). *We Don't Look Like Our Mom and Dad.* Putnam.

Stanley, D. (1996). *The Mulberry Bird: An Adoption Story.* Perspectives Press.

Stinson, K. (1992). *Steven's Baseball Mitt: A Book about Being Adopted.* Annick Press.

Thomas, E. (2004). *The Red Blanket.* Scholastic Press.

Turner, A. (1992). *Through the Moon and Stars and Night Skies.* HarperTrophy.

Wright, Susan. (1995). *Real Sisters.* Gynery Books/Ragweed Press.

DEVELOPMENTALLY APPROPRIATE PRACTICE

NAEYC's first position statement on Developmentally Appropriate Practice had two main motivations:

- The process of accrediting centers required widely accepted and specific definitions of what constituted excellent practices in early childhood education.

- There was a proliferation of programs that had inappropriate practices and expectations for their children, largely based on premature academic learning.

The original position statement did enhance the early childhood profession, although it was not received with universal acceptance. So a revised position statement clarified some of the previous misunderstandings and expanded the vision of good practices.

It is important to keep the principles firmly in mind when making professional decisions. It is also important to use the statement in conversations with others regarding appropriate practices. Colleagues, administrators, and family members all have their individual understandings of what to do with young children. It is, therefore, useful for you as a teacher to get your own copy of the position statement. In a conversation, you can use the position statement to replace the idea of personal opinions with the weight of the professional body of knowledge. For the purpose of this Professional Enhancement text, it is particularly important to note that one of the five teacher roles described by the statement relates to establishing reciprocal relationships with families. Pay particular attention to segment 5 as you read. The complete statement, Developmentally

Appropriate Practice in Early Childhood Programs, Revised Edition (NAEYC 1997), follows:

DEVELOPMENTALLY APPROPRIATE PRACTICE IN EARLY CHILDHOOD PROGRAMS SERVING CHILDREN FROM BIRTH THROUGH AGE 8

A Position Statement for the National Association for the Education of Young Children Adopted July 1996

This statement defines and describes principles of developmentally appropriate practice in early childhood programs for administrators, teachers, parents, policymakers, and others who make decisions about the care and education of young children. An early childhood program is any group program in a center, school, or other facility that serves children from birth through age eight. Early childhood programs include child care centers, family child care homes, private and public preschools, kindergartens, and primary-grade schools.

The early childhood profession is responsible for establishing and promoting standards of high-quality, professional practice in early childhood programs. These standards must reflect current knowledge and shared beliefs about what constitutes high-quality, developmentally appropriate early childhood education in the context within which services are delivered.

This position paper is organized into several components, which include the following:

1. a description of the current context in which early childhood programs operate;

2. a description of the rationale and need for NAEYC's position statement;

3. a statement of NAEYC's commitment to children;

4. the statement of the position and definition of *developmentally appropriate practice*;

5. a summary of the principles of child development and learning and the theoretical perspectives that inform decisions about early childhood practice;

6. guidelines for making decisions about developmentally appropriate practices that address the following integrated components of early childhood practice: creating a caring

community of learners, teaching to enhance children's learning and development, constructing appropriate curriculum, assessing children's learning and development, and establishing reciprocal relationships with families;

7. a challenge to the field to move from *either/or* to *both/and* thinking; and

8. recommendations for policies necessary to ensure developmentally appropriate practices for all children.

This statement is designed to be used in conjunction with NAEYC's "Criteria for High Quality Early Childhood Programs," the standards for accreditation by the National Academy of Early Childhood Programs (NAEYC 1991), and with "Guidelines for Appropriate Curriculum Content and Assessment in Programs Serving Children Ages 3 through 8" (NAEYC & NAECS/SDE 1992; Bredekamp & Rosegrant 1992, 1995).

The Current Context of Early Childhood Programs

The early childhood knowledge base has expanded considerably in recent years, affirming some of the profession's cherished beliefs about good practice and challenging others. In addition to gaining new knowledge, early childhood programs have experienced several important changes in recent years. The number of programs continues to increase not only in response to the growing demand for out-of-home child care but also in recognition of the critical importance of educational experiences during the early years (Willer et al. 1991; NCES 1993). For example, in the late 1980s Head Start embarked on the largest expansion in its history, continuing this expansion into the 1990s with significant new services for families with infants and toddlers. The National Education Goals Panel established as an objective of Goal 1 that by the year 2000 all children will have access to high-quality, developmentally appropriate preschool programs (NEGP 1991). Welfare reform portends a greatly increased demand for child care services for even the youngest children from very-low-income families.

Some characteristics of early childhood programs have also changed in recent years. Increasingly, programs serve children and families from diverse cultural and linguistic backgrounds, requiring that all programs demonstrate understanding of and responsiveness to cultural and linguistic diversity. Because culture and language are critical components of children's development, practices cannot be developmentally appropriate unless they are responsive to cultural and linguistic diversity.

The Americans with Disabilities Act and the Individuals with Disabilities Education Act now require that all early childhood programs make reasonable accommodations to provide access for children with disabilities or developmental delays (DEC/CEC & NAEYC 1993). This legal right reflects the growing consensus that young children with disabilities are best served in the same community settings where their typically developing peers are found (DEC/CEC 1994).

The trend toward full inclusion of children with disabilities must be reflected in descriptions of recommended practices, and considerable work has been done toward converging the perspectives of early childhood and early childhood special education (Carta, Schwartz, Atwater, & McConnell 1991; Mallory 1992, 1994; Wolery, Strain, & Bailey 1992; Bredekamp 1993b; DEC Task Force 1993; Mallory & New 1994b; Wolery & Wilbers 1994).

Other important program characteristics include age of children and length of program day. Children are now enrolled in programs at younger ages, many from infancy. The length of the program day for all ages of children has been extended in response to the need for extended hours of care for employed families. Similarly, program sponsorship has become more diverse. The public schools in the majority of states now provide pre-kindergarten programs, some for children as young as three, and many offer before- and after-school child care (Mitchell, Seligson, & Marx 1989; Seppanen, Kaplan deVries, & Seligson 1993; Adams & Sandfort 1994).

Corporate America has become a more visible sponsor of child care programs, with several key corporations leading the way in promoting high quality (for example, IBM, AT&T, and the American Business Collaboration). Family child care homes have become an increasingly visible sector of the child care community, with greater emphasis on professional development and the National Association for Family Child Care taking the lead in establishing an accreditation system for high-quality family child care (Hollestelle 1993; Cohen & Modigliani 1994; Galinsky, Howes, Kontos, & Shinn 1994). Many different settings in this country provide services to young children, and it is legitimate—even beneficial—for these settings to vary in certain ways. However, since it is vital to meet children's learning and developmental needs wherever they are served, high standards of quality should apply to all settings.

The context in which early childhood programs operate today is also characterized by ongoing debates about how best to teach young children and discussions about what sort of practice is most likely to contribute to their development and learning. Perhaps the most important contribution of NAEYC's 1987 position statement on developmentally appropriate practice (Bredekamp 1987) was that it created an opportunity for increased conversation within and outside the early childhood field about practices. In revising the position statement, NAEYC's goal is not only to improve the quality of current early childhood practice but also to continue to encourage the kind of questioning and debate among early childhood professionals that are necessary for the continued growth of professional knowledge in the field. A related goal is to express NAEYC's position more clearly so that energy is not wasted in unproductive debate about apparent rather than real differences of opinion.

Rationale for the Position Statement

The increased demand for early childhood education services is partly due to the increased recognition of the crucial importance of experiences during the earliest years of life. Children's experiences during early childhood not only influence their later functioning in school but can have effects throughout life. For example, current research demonstrates the early and lasting effects of children's environments and experiences on brain development and cognition (Chugani, Phelps, & Mazziotta 1987; Caine & Caine 1991; Kuhl 1994). Studies show that, "From infancy through about age 10, brain cells not only form most of the connections they will maintain throughout life but during this time they retain their greatest malleability" (Dana Alliance for Brain Initiatives 1996, 7).

Positive, supportive relationships, important during the earliest years of life, appear essential not only for cognitive development but also for healthy emotional development and social attachment (Bowlby 1969; Stern 1985). The preschool years are an optimum time for development of fundamental motor skills (Gallahue 1993), language development (Dyson & Genishi 1993), and other key foundational aspects of development that have lifelong implications.

Recognition of the importance of the early years has heightened interest and support for early childhood education programs.

A number of studies demonstrating long-term, positive consequences of participation in high-quality early childhood programs
for children from low-income families influenced the expansion of
Head Start and public school prekindergarten (Lazar & Darlington
1982; Lee, Brooks-Gunn, & Schuur 1988; Schweinhart, Barnes, &
Weikart 1993; Campbell & Ramey 1995). Several decades of research clearly demonstrate that high-quality, developmentally appropriate early childhood programs produce short- and long-term
positive effects on children's cognitive and social development (Barnett
1995).

From a thorough review of the research on the long-term effects of early childhood education programs, Barnett concludes that
"across all studies, the findings were relatively uniform and consti-
tute overwhelming evidence that early childhood care and education can produce sizeable improvements in school success" (1995,
40). Children from low-income families who participated in high-
quality preschool programs were significantly less likely to have
been assigned to special education, retained in grade, engaged in
crime, or to have dropped out of school. The longitudinal studies,
in general, suggest positive consequences for programs that used an
approach consistent with principles of developmentally appropriate
practice (Lazar & Darlington 1982; Berruetta-Clement, Schweinhart,
Barnett, Epstein, & Weikart 1984; Miller & Bizzell 1984; Schweinhart, Weikart, & Larner 1986; Schweinhart, Barnes, & Weikart
1993; Frede 1995; Schweinhart & Weikart 1996).

Research on the long-term effects of early childhood programs indicates that children who attend good-quality child care
programs, even at very young ages, demonstrate positive outcomes,
and children who attend poor-quality programs show negative effects (Vandell & Powers 1983; Phillips, McCartney, & Scarr 1987;
Fields, Masi, Goldstein, Perry, & Parl 1988; Vandell, Henderson, &
Wilson 1988; Arnett 1989; Vandell & Corasanti 1990; Burchinal,
Robert, Nabo, & Bryant 1996). Specifically, children who experience high-quality, stable child care engage in more complex play,
demonstrate more secure attachments to adults and other children,
and score higher on measures of thinking ability and language development. High-quality child care can predict academic success,
adjustment to school, and reduced behavioral problems for children in first grade (Howes 1988).

While the potential positive effects of high-quality child care are well documented, several large-scale evaluations of child care find that high-quality experiences are not the norm (Whitebook, Howes, & Phillips 1989; Howes, Phillips, & Whitebook 1992; Layzer, Goodson, & Moss 1993; Galinsky et al. 1994; Cost, Quality, & Child Outcomes Study Team 1995). Each of these studies, which included observations of child care and preschool quality in several states, found that good quality that supports children's health and social and cognitive development is being provided in only about 15 percent of programs.

Of even greater concern was the large percentage of classrooms and family child care homes that were rated "barely adequate" or "inadequate" for quality. From 12 to 20 percent of the children were in settings that were considered dangerous to their health and safety and harmful to their social and cognitive development. An alarming number of infants and toddlers (35 to 40 percent) were found to be in unsafe settings (Cost, Quality, & Child Outcomes Study Team 1995).

Experiences during the earliest years of formal schooling are also formative. Studies demonstrate that children's success or failure during the first years of school often predicts the course of later schooling (Alexander & Entwisle 1988; Slavin, Karweit, & Madden 1989). A growing body of research indicates that more developmentally appropriate teaching in preschool and kindergarten predicts greater success in the early grades (Frede & Barnett 1992; Marcon 1992; Charlesworth, Hart, Burts, & DeWolf 1993).

As with preschool and child care, the observed quality of children's early schooling is uneven (Durkin 1987, 1990; Hiebert & Papierz 1990; Bryant, Clifford, & Peisner 1991; Carnegie Task Force 1996). For instance, in a statewide observational study of kindergarten classrooms, Durkin (1987) found that despite assessment results indicating considerable individual variation in children's literacy skills, which would call for various teaching strategies as well as individual and small-group work, teachers relied on one instructional strategy—whole-group, phonics instruction—and judged children who did not learn well with this one method as unready for first grade. Currently, too many children—especially children from low-income families and some minority groups—experience school failure, are retained in grade, get assigned to special education, and eventually drop out of school (Natriello, McDill, & Pallas 1990; Legters & Slavin 1992).

Results such as these indicate that while early childhood programs have the potential for producing positive and lasting effects on children, this potential will not be achieved unless more attention is paid to ensuring that all programs meet the highest standards of quality. As the number and type of early childhood programs increase, the need increases for a shared vision and agreed-upon standards of professional practice.

NAEYC's Commitment to Children

It is important to acknowledge at the outset the core values that undergird all of NAEYC's work. As stated in NAEYC's *Code of Ethical Conduct,* standards of professional practice in early childhood programs are based on commitment to certain fundamental values that are deeply rooted in the history of the early childhood field:

- appreciating childhood as a unique and valuable stage of the human life cycle (and valuing the quality of children's lives in the present, not just as preparation for the future);

- basing our work with children on knowledge of child development (and learning);

- appreciating and supporting the close ties between the child and family;

- recognizing that children are best understood in the context of family, culture, and society;

- respecting the dignity, worth, and uniqueness of each individual (child, family member, and colleague); and

- helping children and adults achieve their full potential in the context of relationships that are based on trust, respect, and positive regard. (Feeney & Kipnis 1992, 3)

Statement of the Position

Based on an enduring commitment to act on behalf of children, NAEYC's mission is to promote high-quality, developmentally appropriate programs for all children and their families. Because we define developmentally appropriate programs as programs that contribute to children's development, we must articulate our goals for children's development. The principles of practice advocated in this position statement are based on a set of goals for children: what we want for them, both in their present lives and as they develop to adulthood, and what personal characteristics should be fostered because these contribute to a peaceful, prosperous, and democratic society.

As we approach the 21st century, enormous changes are taking place in daily life and work. At the same time, certain human capacities will undoubtedly remain important elements in individual and societal well-being—no matter what economic or technological changes take place. With a recognition of both the continuities in human existence and the rapid changes in our world, broad agreement is emerging (e.g., Resnick 1996) that when today's children become adults they will need the ability to:

- communicate well, respect others and engage with them to work through differences of opinion, and function well as members of a team;

- analyze situations, make reasoned judgments, and solve new problems as they emerge;

- access information through various modes, including spoken and written language, and intelligently employ complex tools and technologies as they are developed; and

- continue to learn new approaches, skills, and knowledge as conditions and needs change.

Clearly, people in the decades ahead will need, more than ever, fully developed literacy and numeracy skills, and these abilities are key goals of the educational process. In science, social studies (which includes history and geography), music and the visual arts, physical education and health, children need to acquire a body of knowledge and skills, as identified by those in the various disciplines (e.g., Bredekamp & Rosegrant 1995).

Besides acquiring a body of knowledge and skills, children must develop positive dispositions and attitudes. They need to understand that effort is necessary for achievement, for example, and they need to have curiosity and confidence in themselves as learners. Moreover, to live in a highly pluralistic society and world, young people need to develop a positive self-identity and a tolerance for others whose perspective and experience may be different from their own.

Beyond the shared goals of the early childhood field, every program for young children should establish its own goals in collaboration with families. All early childhood programs will not have identical goals; priorities may vary in some respects because programs serve a diversity of children and families. Such differences notwithstanding, NAEYC believes that all high-quality, developmentally appropriate programs will have certain attributes in common. A high-quality early childhood program is one that provides a safe and nurturing environment that promotes the physical, social, emotional, aesthetic, intellectual, and language development of each child while being sensitive to the needs and preferences of families.

Many factors influence the quality of an early childhood program, including (but not limited to) the extent to which knowledge about how children develop and learn is applied in program practices. Developmentally appropriate programs are based on what is known about how children develop and learn; such programs promote the development and enhance the learning of each individual child served.

Developmentally appropriate practices result from the process of professionals making decisions about the well-being and education of children based on at least three important kinds of information or knowledge:

1. *what is known about child development and learning—* knowledge of age-related human characteristics that permits general predictions within an age range about what activities, materials, interactions, or experiences will be safe, healthy, interesting, achievable, and also challenging to children;

2. *what is known about the strengths, interests, and needs of each individual child in the group* to be able to adapt for and be responsive to inevitable individual variation; and

3. *knowledge of the social and cultural contexts in which children live* to ensure that learning experiences are meaningful, relevant, and respectful for the participating children and their families.

Furthermore, each of these dimensions of knowledge—human development and learning, individual characteristics and experiences, and social and cultural contexts—is dynamic and changing, requiring that early childhood teachers remain learners throughout their careers.

An example illustrates the interrelatedness of these three dimensions of the decision-making process. Children all over the world acquire language at approximately the same period of the life span and in similar ways (Fernald 1992). But tremendous individual variation exists in the rate and pattern of language acquisition (Fenson et al. 1994). Also, children acquire the language or languages of the culture in which they live (Kuhl 1994). Thus, to adequately support a developmental task such as language acquisition, the teacher must draw on at least all three interrelated dimensions of knowledge to determine a developmentally appropriate strategy or intervention.

Principles of Child Development and Learning that Inform Developmentally Appropriate Practice

Taken together, these core values define NAEYC's basic commitment to children and underlie its position on developmentally appropriate practice.

Developmentally appropriate practice is based on knowledge about how children develop and learn. As Katz states, "In a developmental approach to curriculum design, . . . [decisions] about what should be learned and how it would best be learned depend on what we know of the learner's developmental status and our understanding of the relationships between early experience and subsequent development" (1995, 109). To guide their decisions about practice, all early childhood teachers need to understand the developmental changes that typically occur in the years from birth through age eight and beyond, variations in development that may occur, and how best to support children's learning and development during these years.

A complete discussion of the knowledge base that informs early childhood practice is beyond the scope of this document (see, for example, Seefeldt 1992; Sroufe, Cooper, & DeHart 1992; Kostelnik, Soderman, & Whiren 1993; Spodek 1993; Berk 1996). Because development and learning are so complex, no one theory is sufficient to explain these phenomena. However, a broad-based review of the literature on early childhood education generates a set of principles to inform early childhood practice. *Principles* are generalizations that are sufficiently reliable that they should be taken into account when making decisions (Katz & Chard 1989; Katz 1995). Following is a list of empirically based principles of child development and learning that inform and guide decisions about developmentally appropriate practice.

1. Domains of children's development—physical, social, emotional, and cognitive—are closely related. Development in one domain influences and is influenced by development in other domains.

Development in one domain can limit or facilitate development in others (Sroufe, Cooper, & DeHart 1992; Kostelnik, Soderman, & Whiren 1993). For example, when babies begin to crawl or walk, their ability to explore the world expands, and their mobility, in turn, affects their cognitive development. Likewise, children's language skill affects their ability to establish social relationships with adults and other children, just as their skill in social interaction can support or impede their language development. Because developmental domains are interrelated, educators should be aware of and use these interrelationships to organize children's learning experiences in ways that help children develop optimally in all areas and that make meaningful connections across domains. Recognition of the connections across developmental domains is also useful for curriculum planning with the various age groups represented in the early childhood period. Curriculum with infants and toddlers is almost solely driven by the need to support their healthy development in all domains. During the primary grades, curriculum planning attempts to help children develop conceptual understandings that apply across related subject-matter disciplines.

2. Development occurs in a relatively orderly sequence, with later abilities, skills, and knowledge building on those already acquired.

Human development research indicates that relatively stable, predictable sequences of growth and change occur in children during the first nine years of life (Piaget 1952; Erikson 1963; Dyson & Genishi 1993; Gallahue 1993; Case & Okamoto 1996). Predictable changes occur in all domains of development—physical, emotional, social, language, and cognitive—although the ways that these changes are manifest and the meaning attached to them may vary in different cultural contexts. Knowledge of typical development of children within the age span served by the program provides a general framework to guide how teachers prepare the learning environment and plan realistic curriculum goals and objectives and appropriate experiences.

3. Development proceeds at varying rates from child to child as well as unevenly within different areas of each child's functioning.

Individual variation has at least two dimensions: the inevitable variability around the average or normative course of development and the uniqueness of each person as an individual (Sroufe, Cooper, & DeHart 1992). Each child is a unique person with an individual pattern and timing of growth, as well as individual personality, temperament, learning style, and experiential and family background. All children have their own strengths, needs, and interests; for some children, special learning and developmental needs or abilities are identified. Given the enormous variation among children of the same chronological age, a child's age must be recognized as only a crude index of developmental maturity.

Recognition that individual variation is not only to be expected but also valued requires that decisions about curriculum and adults' interactions with children be as individualized as possible. Emphasis on individual appropriateness is not the same as "individualism." Rather, this recognition requires that children be considered not solely as members of an age group, expected to perform to a predetermined norm and without adaptation to individual variation of any kind. Having high expectations for all children is important, but rigid expectations of group norms do not reflect what is known about real differences in individual development and learning during the early years. Group-norm expectancy can be especially harmful for children with special learning and developmental needs (NEGP 1991; Mallory 1992; Wolery, Strain, & Bailey 1992).

4. Early experiences have both cumulative and delayed effects on individual children's development; optimal periods exist for certain types of development and learning.

Children's early experiences, either positive or negative, are cumulative in the sense that if an experience occurs occasionally, it may have minimal effects. If positive or negative experiences occur frequently, however, they can have powerful, lasting, even "snow-balling," effects (Katz & Chard 1989; Kostelnik, Soderman, & Whiren 1993; Wieder & Greenspan 1993). For example, a child's social experiences with other children in the preschool years help him develop social skills and confidence that enable him to make friends in the early school years, and these experiences further enhance the child's social competence. Conversely, children who fail to develop minimal social competence and are neglected or rejected by peers are at significant risk to drop out of school, become delinquent, and experience mental health problems in adulthood (Asher, Hymel, & Renshaw 1984; Parker & Asher 1987).

Similar patterns can be observed in babies whose cries and other attempts at communication are regularly responded to, thus enhancing their own sense of efficacy and increasing communicative competence. Likewise, when children have or do not have early literacy experiences, such as being read to regularly, their later success in learning to read is affected accordingly. Perhaps most convincing is the growing body of research demonstrating that social and sensorimotor experiences during the first three years directly affect neurological development of the brain, with important and lasting implications for children's capacity to learn (Dana Alliance for Brain Initiatives 1996).

Early experiences can also have delayed effects, either positive or negative, on subsequent development. For instance, some evidence suggests that reliance on extrinsic rewards (such as candy or money) to shape children's behavior, a strategy that can be very effective in the short term, under certain circumstances lessens children's intrinsic motivation to engage in the rewarded behavior in the long term (Dweck 1986; Kohn 1993). For example, paying children to read books may over time undermine their desire to read for their own enjoyment and edification.

At certain points in the life span, some kinds of learning and development occur most efficiently. For example, the first three years of life appear to be an optimal period for verbal language development (Kuhl 1994). Although delays in language development due to physical or environmental deficits can be ameliorated later on, such intervention usually requires considerable effort. Similarly, the preschool years appear to be optimum for fundamental motor development (that is, fundamental motor skills are more easily and efficiently acquired at this age) (Gallahue 1995). Children who have many opportunities and adult support to practice large motor skills (running, jumping, hopping, skipping) during this period have the cumulative benefit of being better able to acquire more sophisticated, complex motor skills (balancing on a beam or riding a two-wheel bike) in subsequent years. On the other hand, children whose early motor experiences are severely limited may struggle to acquire physical competence and may also experience delayed effects when attempting to participate in sports or personal fitness activities later in life.

5. Development proceeds in predictable directions toward greater complexity, organization, and internalization.

Learning during early childhood proceeds from behavioral knowledge to symbolic or representational knowledge (Bruner 1983). For example, children learn to navigate their homes and other familiar settings long before they can understand the words *left* and *right* or read a map of the house. Developmentally appropriate programs provide opportunities for children to broaden and deepen their behavioral knowledge by providing a variety of firsthand experiences and by helping children acquire symbolic knowledge through representing their experiences in a variety of media, such as drawing, painting, construction of models, dramatic play, verbal and written descriptions (Katz 1995).

Even very young children are able to use various media to represent their understanding of concepts. Furthermore, through representation of their knowledge, the knowledge itself is enhanced (Edwards, Gandini, & Forman 1993; Malaguzzi 1993; Forman 1994). Representational modes and media also vary with the age of the child. For instance, most learning for infants and toddlers is sensory and motoric, but by age two children use one object to stand for another in play (a block for a phone or a spoon for a guitar).

6. Development and learning occur in and are influenced by multiple social and cultural contexts.

Bronfenbrenner (1979, 1989, 1993) provides an ecological model for understanding human development. He explains that children's development is best understood within the sociocultural context of the family, educational setting, community, and broader society. These various contexts are interrelated, and all have an impact on the developing child. For example, even a child in a loving, supportive family within a strong, healthy community is affected by the biases of the larger society, such as racism or sexism, and may show the effects of negative stereotyping and discrimination.

We define *culture* as the customary beliefs and patterns of and for behavior, both explicit and implicit, that are passed on to future generations by the society they live in and/or by a social, religious, or ethnic group within it. Because culture is often discussed in the context of diversity or multiculturalism, people fail to recognize the powerful role that culture plays in influencing the development of *all* children. Every culture structures and interprets children's behavior and development (Edwards & Gandini 1989; Tobin, Wu, & Davidson 1989; Rogoff, Mistry, Goncu, & Mosier 1993). As Bowman states, "Rules of development are the same for all children, but social contexts shape children's development into different configurations" (1994, 220). Early childhood teachers need to understand the influence of sociocultural contexts on learning, recognize children's developing competence, and accept a variety of ways for children to express their developmental achievements (Vygotsky 1978; Wertsch 1985; Forman, Minick, & Stone 1993; New 1993, 1994; Bowman & Stott 1994; Mallory & New 1994a; Phillips 1994; Bruner 1996; Wardle 1996).

Teachers should learn about the culture of the majority of the children they serve if that culture differs from their own. However, recognizing that development and learning are influenced by social and cultural contexts does not require teachers to understand all the nuances of every cultural group they may encounter in their practice; this would be an impossible task. Rather, this fundamental recognition sensitizes teachers to the need to acknowledge how their own cultural experience shapes their perspective and to realize that multiple perspectives, in addition to their own, must be considered in decisions about children's development and learning.

Children are capable of learning to function in more than one cultural context simultaneously. However, if teachers set low expectations for children based on their home culture and language, children cannot develop and learn optimally. Education should be an additive process. For example, children whose primary language is not English should be able to learn English without being forced to give up their home language (NAEYC 1996a). Likewise, children who speak only English benefit from learning another language.

The goal is that all children learn to function well in the society as a whole and move comfortably among groups of people who come from both similar and dissimilar backgrounds.

7. Children are active learners, drawing on direct physical and social experience as well as culturally transmitted knowledge to construct their own understandings of the world around them.

Children contribute to their own development and learning as they strive to make meaning out of their daily experiences in the home, the early childhood program, and the community. Principles of developmentally appropriate practice are based on several prominent theories that view intellectual development from a constructivist, interactive perspective (Dewey 1916; Piaget 1952; Vygotsky 1978; DeVries & Kohlberg 1990; Rogoff 1990; Gardner 1991; Kamii & Ewing 1996).

From birth, children are actively engaged in constructing their own understandings from their experiences, and these understandings are mediated by and clearly linked to the sociocultural context. Young children actively learn from observing and participating with other children and adults, including parents and teachers. Children need to form their own hypotheses and keep trying them out through social interaction, physical manipulation, and their own thought processes—observing what happens, reflecting on their findings, asking questions, and formulating answers. When objects, events, and other people challenge the working model that the child has mentally constructed, the child is forced to adjust the model or alter the mental structures to account for the new information. Throughout early childhood, the child in processing new experiences continually reshapes, expands, and reorganizes mental structures (Piaget 1952; Vygotsky 1978; Case & Okamoto 1996). When teachers and other adults use various strategies to encourage children to reflect on their experiences by planning beforehand and "revisiting" afterward, the knowledge and understanding gained from the experience is deepened (Copple, Sigel, & Saunders 1984; Edwards, Gandini, & Forman 1993; Stremmel & Fu 1993; Hohmann & Weikart 1995).

In the statement of this principle, the term "physical and social experience" is used in the broadest sense to include children's exposure to physical knowledge, learned through firsthand experience of using objects (observing that a ball thrown in the air falls down), and social knowledge, including the vast body of culturally acquired and transmitted knowledge that children need to function in the world. For example, children progressively construct their own understanding of various symbols, but the symbols they use (such as the alphabet or numerical system) are the ones used within their culture and transmitted to them by adults.

In recent years, discussions of cognitive development have at times become polarized (see Seifert 1993). Piaget's theory stressed that development of certain cognitive structures was a necessary prerequisite to learning (i.e., development precedes learning), while other research has demonstrated that instruction in specific concepts or strategies can facilitate development of more mature cognitive structures (learning precedes development) (Vygotsky 1978; Gelman & Baillargeon 1983). Current attempts to resolve this apparent dichotomy (Seifert 1993; Sameroff & McDonough 1994; Case & Okamoto 1996) acknowledge that essentially both theoretical perspectives are correct in explaining aspects of cognitive development during early childhood. Strategic teaching, of course, can enhance children's learning. Yet, direct instruction may be totally ineffective; it fails when it is not attuned to the cognitive capacities and knowledge of the child at that point in development.

8. Development and learning result from interaction of biological maturation and the environment, which includes both the physical and social worlds that children live in.

The simplest way to express this principle is that human beings are products of both heredity and environment and these forces are interrelated. Behaviorists focus on the environmental influences that determine learning, while maturationists emphasize the unfolding of predetermined, hereditary characteristics. Each perspective is true to some extent, and yet neither perspective is sufficient to explain learning or development. More often today, development is viewed as the result of an interactive, transactional process between the growing, changing individual and his or her experiences in the social and physical worlds (Scarr & McCartney 1983; Plomin 1994a, b). For example, a child's genetic makeup may predict healthy growth, but inadequate nutrition in the early years of life may keep this potential from being fulfilled. Or a severe disability, whether inherited or environmentally caused, may be ameliorated through systematic, appropriate intervention. Likewise, a child's in-

herited temperament—whether a predisposition to be wary or out-
going—shapes and is shaped by how other children and adults
communicate with that child.

**9. Play is an important vehicle for children's social,
emotional, and cognitive development, as well as a reflection
of their development.**

Understanding that children are active constructors of knowledge and that development and learning are the result of interactive
processes, early childhood teachers recognize that children's play is
a highly supportive context for these developing processes (Piaget
1952; Fein 1981; Bergen 1988; Smilansky & Shefatya 1990;
Fromberg 1992; Berk & Winsler 1995). Play gives children opportunities to understand the world, interact with others in social ways,
express and control emotions, and develop their symbolic capabilities. Children's play gives adults insights into children's development and opportunities to support the development of new
strategies. Vygotsky (1978) believed that play leads development,
with written language growing out of oral language through the vehicle of symbolic play that promotes the development of symbolic
representation abilities. Play provides a context for children to practice newly acquired skills and also to function on the edge of their
developing capacities to take on new social roles, attempt novel or
challenging tasks, and solve complex problems that they would not
(or could not) otherwise do (Mallory & New 1994b).

Research demonstrates the importance of sociodramatic play
as a tool for learning curriculum content with three- through six-
year-old children. When teachers provide a thematic organization
for play; offer appropriate props, space, and time; and become involved in the play by extending and elaborating on children's ideas,
children's language and literacy skills can be enhanced (Levy, Schaefer,
& Phelps 1986; Schrader 1989, 1990; Morrow 1990; Pramling
1991; Levy, Wolfgang, & Koorland 1992).

In addition to supporting cognitive development, play serves
important functions in children's physical, emotional, and social development (Herron & Sutton-Smith 1971). Children express and
represent their ideas, thoughts, and feelings when engaged in symbolic play. During play a child can learn to deal with emotions, to interact with others, to resolve conflicts, and to gain a sense of
competence—all in the safety that only play affords. Through play,

children also can develop their imaginations and creativity. There-fore, child-initiated, teacher-supported play is an essential compo-nent of developmentally appropriate practice (Fein & Rivkin 1986).

10. Development advances when children have opportunities to practice newly acquired skills as well as when they experience a challenge just beyond the level of their present mastery.

Research demonstrates that children need to be able to suc-cessfully negotiate learning tasks most of the time if they are to maintain motivation and persistence (Lary 1990; Brophy 1992). Confronted by repeated failure, most children will simply stop try-ing. So most of the time, teachers should give young children tasks that with effort they can accomplish and present them with content that is accessible at their level of understanding. At the same time, children continually gravitate to situations and stimuli that give them the chance to work at their "growing edge" (Berk & Winsler 1995; Bodrova & Leong 1996). Moreover, in a task just beyond the child's independent reach, the adult and more-competent peers contribute significantly to development by providing the support-ive "scaffolding" that allows the child to take the next step.

Development and learning are dynamic processes requiring that adults understand the continuum, observe children closely to match curriculum and teaching to children's emerging competen-cies, needs, and interests, and then help children move forward by targeting educational experiences to the edge of children's changing capacities so as to challenge but not frustrate them. Human beings, especially children, are highly motivated to understand what they al-most, but not quite, comprehend and to master what they can al-most, but not quite, do (White 1965; Vygotsky 1978). The principle of learning is that children can do things first in a supportive context and then later independently and in a variety of contexts. Rogoff (1990) describes the process of adult-assisted learning as "guided participation" to emphasize that children actively collaborate with others to move to more complex levels of understanding and skill.

11. Children demonstrate different modes of knowing and learning and different ways of representing what they know.

For some time, learning theorists and developmental psy-chologists have recognized that human beings come to understand the world in many ways and that individuals tend to have preferred or stronger modes of learning. Studies of differences in learning modalities have contrasted visual, auditory, or tactile learners. Other work has identified learners as field-dependent or independent (Witkin 1962). Gardner (1983) expanded on this concept by theorizing that human beings possess at least seven "intelligences." In addition to having the ones traditionally emphasized in schools, linguistic and logical-mathematical, individuals are more or less proficient in at least these other areas: musical, spatial, bodily-kinesthetic, intrapersonal, and interpersonal.

Malaguzzi (1993) used the metaphor of "100 languages" to describe the diverse modalities through which children come to understand the world and represent their knowledge. The processes of representing their understanding can with the assistance of teachers help children deepen, improve, and expand their understanding (Copple, Sigel, & Saunders 1984; Forman 1994; Katz 1995). The principle of diverse modalities implies that teachers should provide not only opportunities for individual children to use their preferred modes of learning to capitalize on their strengths (Hale-Benson 1986) but also opportunities to help children develop in the modes or intelligences in which they may not be as strong.

12. Children develop and learn best in the context of a community where they are safe and valued, their physical needs are met, and they feel psychologically secure.

Maslow (1954) conceptualized a hierarchy of needs in which learning was not considered possible unless physical and psychological needs for safety and security were first met. Because children's physical health and safety too often are threatened today, programs for young children must not only provide adequate health, safety, and nutrition but may also need to ensure more comprehensive services, such as physical, dental, and mental health and social services (NASBE 1991; U.S. Department of Health & Human Services 1996). In addition, children's development in all areas is influenced by their ability to establish and maintain a limited number of positive, consistent primary relationships with adults and other children (Bowlby 1969; Stern 1985; Garbarino, Dubrow, Kostelny, & Pardo 1992). These primary relationships begin in the family but extend over time to include children's teachers and members of the community; therefore, practices that are developmentally appropriate address children's physical, social, and emotional needs as well as their intellectual development.

Guidelines for Decisions about Developmentally Appropriate Practice

A linear listing of principles of child development and learning, such as the above, cannot do justice to the complexity of the phenomena that it attempts to describe and explain. Just as all domains of development and learning are interrelated, so, too, there are relationships among the principles. Similarly, the following guidelines for practice do not match up one-to-one with the principles. Instead, early childhood professionals draw on all these fundamental ideas (as well as many others) when making decisions about their practice.

An understanding of the nature of development and learning during the early childhood years, from birth through age eight, generates guidelines that inform the practices of early childhood educators. Developmentally appropriate practice requires that teachers integrate the many dimensions of their knowledge base. They must know about child development and the implications of this knowledge for how to teach, the content of the curriculum—what to teach and when—how to assess what children have learned, and how to adapt curriculum and instruction to children's individual strengths, needs, and interests. Further, they must know the particular children they teach and their families and be knowledgeable as well about the social and cultural context.

The following guidelines address five interrelated dimensions of early childhood professional practice: creating a caring community of learners, teaching to enhance development and learning, constructing appropriate curriculum, assessing children's development and learning, and establishing reciprocal relationships with families. (The word *teacher* is used to refer to any adult responsible for a group of children in any early childhood program, including infant/toddler caregivers, family child care providers, and specialists in other disciplines who fulfill the role of teacher.)

Examples of appropriate and inappropriate practice in relation to each of these dimensions are given for infants and toddlers (Part 3, pp. 72–90), children three through five (Part 4, pp. 123–35), and children six through eight (Part 5, pp. 161–78). In the references at the end of each part, readers will be able to find fuller discussion of the points summarized here and strategies for implementation.

1. Creating a caring community of learners

Developmentally appropriate practices occur within a context that supports the development of relationships between adults and children, among children, among teachers, and between teachers and families. Such a community reflects what is known about the social construction of knowledge and the importance of establishing a caring, inclusive community in which all children can develop and learn.

A. The early childhood setting functions as a community of learners in which all participants consider and contribute to each other's well-being and learning.

B. Consistent, positive relationships with a limited number of adults and other children are a fundamental determinant of healthy human development and provide the context for children to learn about themselves and their world and also how to develop positive, constructive relationships with other people. The early childhood classroom is a community in which each child is valued. Children learn to respect and acknowledge differences in abilities and talents and to value each person for his or her strengths.

C. Social relationships are an important context for learning. Each child has strengths or interests that contribute to the overall functioning of the group. When children have opportunities to play together, work on projects in small groups, and talk with other children and adults, their own development and learning are enhanced. Interacting with other children in small groups provides a context for children to operate on the edge of their developing capacities. The learning environment enables children to construct understanding through interactions with adults and other children.

D. The learning environment is designed to protect children's health and safety and is supportive of children's physiological needs for activity, sensory stimulation, fresh air, rest, and nourishment. The program provides a balance of rest and active movement for children throughout the program day. Outdoor experiences are provided for children of all ages. The program protects children's psychological safety; that is, children feel secure, relaxed, and comfortable rather than disengaged, frightened, worried, or stressed.

E. Children experience an organized environment and an orderly routine that provides an overall structure in which learning takes place; the environment is dynamic and changing but predictable and comprehensible from a child's point of view. The learning environment provides a variety of materials and opportunities for children to have firsthand, meaningful experiences.

2. Teaching to enhance development and learning

Adults are responsible for ensuring children's healthy development and learning. From birth, relationships with adults are critical determinants of children's healthy social and emotional development and serve as well as mediators of language and intellectual development. At the same time, children are active constructors of their own understanding, who benefit from initiating and regulating their own learning activities and interacting with peers. Therefore, early childhood teachers strive to achieve an optimal balance between children's self-initiated learning and adult guidance or support.

Teachers accept responsibility for actively supporting children's development and provide occasions for children to acquire important knowledge and skills. Teachers use their knowledge of child development and learning to identify the range of activities, materials, and learning experiences that are appropriate for a group or individual child. This knowledge is used in conjunction with knowledge of the context and understanding about individual children's growth patterns, strengths, needs, interests, and experiences to design the curriculum and learning environment and guide teachers' interactions with children. The following guidelines describe aspects of the teachers' role in making decisions about practice:

A. Teachers respect, value, and accept children and treat them with dignity at all times.

B. Teachers make it a priority to know each child well.
    (1) *Teachers establish positive, personal relationships with children to foster the child's development and keep informed about the child's needs and potentials. Teachers listen to children and adapt their responses to children's differing needs, interests, styles, and abilities.*
    (2) *Teachers continually observe children's spontaneous play and interaction with the physical environment and with other*

children to learn about their interests, abilities, and developmental progress. On the basis of this information, teachers plan experiences that enhance children's learning and development.

(3) Understanding that children develop and learn in the context of their families and communities, teachers establish relationships with families that increase their knowledge of children's lives outside the classroom and their awareness of the perspectives and priorities of those individuals most significant in the child's life.

(4) Teachers are alert to signs of undue stress and traumatic events in children's lives and aware of effective strategies to reduce stress and support the development of resilience.

(5) Teachers are responsible at all times for all children under their supervision and plan for children's increasing development of self-regulation abilities.

C. Teachers create an intellectually engaging, responsive environment to promote each child's learning and development.

(1) Teachers use their knowledge about children in general and the particular children in the group as well as their familiarity with what children need to learn and develop in each curriculum area to organize the environment and plan curriculum and teaching strategies.

(2) Teachers provide children with a rich variety of experiences, projects, materials, problems, and ideas to explore and investigate, ensuring that these are worthy of children's attention.

(3) Teachers provide children with opportunities to make meaningful choices and time to explore through active involvement. Teachers offer children the choice to participate in a small-group or a solitary activity, assist and guide children who are not yet able to use and enjoy child-choice activity periods, and provide opportunities for practice of skills as a self-chosen activity.

(4) Teachers organize the daily and weekly schedule and allocate time so as to provide children with extended blocks of time in which to engage in play, projects, and/or study in integrated curriculum.

D. Teachers make plans to enable children to attain key curriculum goals across various disciplines, such as language arts, mathematics, social studies, science, art, music, physical education, and health (see "Constructing appropriate curriculum," pp. 20–21).

(1) *Teachers incorporate a wide variety of experiences, materials and equipment, and teaching strategies in constructing curriculum to accommodate a broad range of children's individual differences in prior experiences, maturation rates, styles of learning, needs, and interests.*

(2) *Teachers bring each child's home culture and language into the shared culture of the school so that the unique contributions of each group are recognized and valued by others.*

(3) *Teachers are prepared to meet identified special needs of individual children, including children with disabilities and those who exhibit unusual interests and skills. Teachers use all the strategies identified here, consult with appropriate specialists, and see that the child gets the specialized services he or she requires.*

E. Teachers foster children's collaboration with peers on interesting, important enterprises.

(1) *Teachers promote children's productive collaboration without taking over to the extent that children lose interest.*

(2) *Teachers use a variety of ways of flexibly grouping children for the purposes of instruction, supporting collaboration among children, and building a sense of community. At various times, children have opportunities to work individually, in small groups, and with the whole group.*

F. Teachers develop, refine, and use a wide repertoire of teaching strategies to enhance children's learning and development.

(1) *To help children develop their initiative, teachers encourage them to choose and plan their own learning activities.*

(2) *Teachers pose problems, ask questions, and make comments and suggestions that stimulate children's thinking and extend their learning.*

(3) *Teachers extend the range of children's interests and the scope of their thought through presenting novel experiences and introducing stimulating ideas, problems, experiences, or hypotheses.*

(4) *To sustain an individual child's effort or engagement in purposeful activities, teachers select from a range of strategies, including but not limited to modeling, demonstrating specific skills, and providing information, focused attention, physical proximity, verbal encouragement, reinforcement and other*

behavioral procedures, as well as additional structure and modification of equipment or schedules as needed.

(5) *Teachers coach and/or directly guide children in the acquisition of specific skills as needed.*

(6) *Teachers calibrate the complexity and challenge of activities to suit children's level of skill and knowledge, increasing the challenge as children gain competence and understanding.*

(7) *Teachers provide cues and other forms of "scaffolding" that enable the child to succeed in a task that is just beyond his or her ability to complete alone.*

(8) *To strengthen children's sense of competence and confidence as learners, motivation to persist, and willingness to take risks, teachers provide experiences for children to be genuinely successful and to be challenged.*

(9) *To enhance children's conceptual understanding, teachers use various strategies that encourage children to reflect on and "revisit" their learning experiences.*

G. Teachers facilitate the development of responsibility and self-regulation in children.

(1) *Teachers set clear, consistent, and fair limits for children's behavior and hold children accountable to standards of acceptable behavior. To the extent that children are able, teachers engage them in developing rules and procedures for behavior of class members.*

(2) *Teachers redirect children to more acceptable behavior or activity or use children's mistakes as learning opportunities, patiently reminding children of rules and their rationale as needed.*

(3) *Teachers listen and acknowledge children's feelings and frustrations, respond with respect, guide children to resolve conflicts, and model skills that help children to solve their own problems.*

3. Constructing appropriate curriculum

The content of the early childhood curriculum is determined by many factors, including the subject matter of the disciplines, social or cultural values, and parental input. In developmentally appropriate programs, decisions about curriculum content also take into consideration the age and experience of the learners. Achieving success for all children depends, among other essentials, on providing a challenging, interesting, developmentally appropriate curriculum. NAEYC does not endorse specific curricula. However, one purpose of these guidelines is as a framework for making decisions about developing curriculum or selecting a curriculum model. Teachers who use a validated curriculum model benefit from the evidence of its effectiveness and the accumulated wisdom and experience of others.

In some respects, the curriculum strategies of many teachers today do not demand enough of children and in other ways demand too much of the wrong thing. On the one hand, narrowing the curriculum to those basic skills that can be easily measured on multiple-choice tests diminishes the intellectual challenge for many children. Such intellectually impoverished curriculum underestimates the true competence of children, which has been demonstrated to be much higher than is often assumed (Gelman & Baillargeon 1983; Gelman & Meck 1983; Edwards, Gandini, & Forman 1993; Resnick 1996). Watered-down, oversimplified curriculum leaves many children unchallenged, bored, uninterested, or unmotivated. In such situations, children's experiences are marked by a great many missed opportunities for learning.

On the other hand, curriculum expectations in the early years of schooling sometimes are not appropriate for the age groups served. When next-grade expectations of mastery of basic skills are routinely pushed down to the previous grade and whole group and teacher-led instruction is the dominant teaching strategy, children who cannot sit still and attend to teacher lectures or who are bored and unchallenged or frustrated by doing workbook pages for long periods of time are mislabeled as immature, disruptive, or unready for school (Shepard & Smith 1988). Constructing appropriate curriculum requires attention to at least the following guidelines for practice:

A. Developmentally appropriate curriculum provides for all areas of a child's development: physical, emotional, social, linguistic, aesthetic, and cognitive.

B. Curriculum includes a broad range of content across disciplines and is socially relevant, intellectually engaging, and personally meaningful to children.

C. Curriculum builds upon what children already know and are able to do (activating prior knowledge) to consolidate their learning and to foster their acquisition of new concepts and skills.

D. Effective curriculum plans frequently integrate across traditional subject-matter divisions to help children make meaningful connections and provide opportunities for rich conceptual development; focusing on one subject is also a valid strategy at times.

E. Curriculum promotes the development of knowledge and understanding, processes and skills, as well as the dispositions to use and apply skills and to go on learning.

F. Curriculum content has intellectual integrity, reflecting the key concepts and tools of inquiry of recognized disciplines in ways that are accessible and achievable for young children, ages three through eight (e.g., Bredekamp & Rosegrant 1992, 1995). Children directly participate in study of the disciplines, for instance, by conducting scientific experiments, writing, performing, solving mathematical problems, collecting and analyzing data, collecting oral history, and performing other roles of experts in the disciplines.

G. Curriculum provides opportunities to support children's home culture and language while also developing all children's abilities to participate in the shared culture of the program and the community.

H. Curriculum goals are realistic and attainable for most children in the designated age range for which they are designed.

I. When used, technology is physically and philosophically integrated in the classroom curriculum and teaching. (See "NAEYC Position Statement: Technology and Young Children—Ages Three through Eight" [NAEYC 1996b].)

4. Assessing children's learning and development

Assessment of individual children's development and learning is essential for planning and implementing appropriate curriculum. In developmentally appropriate programs, assessment and curriculum are integrated, with teachers continually engaging in observational assessment for the purpose of improving teaching and learning.

Accurate assessment of young children is difficult because their development and learning are rapid, uneven, episodic, and embedded within specific cultural and linguistic contexts. Too often, inaccurate and inappropriate assessment measures have been used to label, track, or otherwise harm young children.

Developmentally appropriate assessment practices are based on the following guidelines:

A. Assessment of young children's progress and achievements is ongoing, strategic, and purposeful. The results of assessment are used to benefit children—in adapting curriculum and teaching to meet the developmental and learning needs of children, communicating with the child's family, and evaluating the program's effectiveness for the purpose of improving the program.

B. The content of assessments reflects progress toward important learning and developmental goals. The program has a systematic plan for collecting and using assessment information that is integrated with curriculum planning.

C. The methods of assessment are appropriate to the age and experiences of young children. Therefore, assessment of young children relies heavily on the results of observations of children's development, descriptive data, collections of representative work by children, and demonstrated performance during authentic, not contrived, activities. Input from families as well as children's evaluations of their own work are part of the overall assessment strategy.

D. Assessments are tailored to a specific purpose and used only for the purpose for which they have been demonstrated to produce reliable, valid information.

E. Decisions that have a major impact on children, such as enrollment or placement, are never made on the basis of a single developmental assessment or screening device but are based on multiple sources of relevant information, particularly observations by teachers and parents.

F. To identify children who have special learning or developmental needs and to plan appropriate curriculum and teaching for them, developmental assessments and observations are used.

G. Assessment recognizes individual variation in learners and allows for differences in styles and rates of learning. Assessment takes into consideration such factors as the child's facility in English, stage of language acquisition, and whether the child has had the time and opportunity to develop proficiency in his or her home language as well as in English.

H. Assessment legitimately addresses not only what children can do independently but what they can do with assistance from other children or adults. Teachers study children as individuals as well as in relationship to groups by documenting group projects and other collaborative work. (For a more complete discussion of principles of appropriate assessment, see the position statement *Guidelines for Appropriate Curriculum Content and Assessment for Children Ages 3 through 8* [NAEYC & NAECS/SDE 1992]; see also Shepard 1994.)

5. Establishing reciprocal relationships with families

Developmentally appropriate practices derive from deep knowledge of individual children and the context within which they develop and learn. The younger the child, the more necessary it is for professionals to acquire this knowledge through relationships with children's families. The traditional approach to families has been a parent education orientation in which the professionals see themselves as knowing what is best for children and view parents as needing to be educated. There is also the limited view of parent involvement that sees PTA membership as the primary goal. These approaches do not adequately convey the complexity of the partnership between teachers and parents that is a fundamental element of good practice (Powell 1994).

When the parent education approach is criticized in favor of a more family-centered approach, this shift may be misunderstood to mean that parents dictate all program content and professionals abdicate responsibility, doing whatever parents want regardless of whether professionals agree that it is in children's best interest. Either of these extremes oversimplifies the importance of relationships with families and fails to provide the kind of environment in which parents and professionals work together to achieve shared goals for children; such programs with this focus are characterized by at least the following guidelines for practice:

A. Reciprocal relationships between teachers and families require mutual respect, cooperation, shared responsibility, and negotiation of conflicts toward achievement of shared goals.

B. Early childhood teachers work in collaborative partnerships with families, establishing and maintaining regular, frequent two-way communication with children's parents.

C. Parents are welcome in the program and participate in decisions about their children's care and education. Parents observe and participate and serve in decision-making roles in the program.

D. Teachers acknowledge parents' choices and goals for children and respond with sensitivity and respect to parents' preferences and concerns without abdicating professional responsibility to children.

E. Teachers and parents share their knowledge of the child and understanding of children's development and learning as part of day-to-day communication and planned conferences. Teachers support families in ways that maximally promote family decision-making capabilities and competence.

F. To ensure more accurate and complete information, the program involves families in assessing and planning for individual children.

G. The program links families with a range of services, based on identified resources, priorities, and concerns.

H. Teachers, parents, programs, social service and health agencies, and consultants who may have educational responsibility for the child at different times should, with family participation, share developmental information about children as they pass from one level or program to another.

Moving from Either/or to Both/and Thinking in Early Childhood Practice

Some critical reactions to NAEYC's (1987) position statement on developmentally appropriate practice reflect a recurring tendency in the American discourse on education: the polarizing into *either/or* choices of many questions that are more fruitfully seen as *both/ands*. For example, heated debates have broken out about whether children in the early grades should receive whole language or phonics instruction, when, in fact, the two approaches are quite compatible and most effective in combination.

It is true that there are practices that are clearly inappropriate for early childhood professionals—use of physical punishment or disparaging verbal comments about children, discriminating against children or their families, and many other examples that could be cited (see Parts 3, 4, and 5 for examples relevant to different age groups). However, most questions about practice require more complex responses. It is not that children need food or water; they need both.

To illustrate the many ways that early childhood practice draws on *both/and* thinking and to convey some of the complexity and interrelationship among the principles that guide our practice, we offer the following statements as examples:

- Children construct their own understanding of concepts, and they benefit from instruction by more competent peers and adults.

- Children benefit from opportunities to see connections across disciplines through integration of curriculum and from opportunities to engage in in-depth study within a content area.

- Children benefit from predictable structure and orderly routine in the learning environment and from the teacher's flexibility and spontaneity in responding to their emerging ideas, needs, and interests.

- Children benefit from opportunities to make meaningful choices about what they will do and learn and from having a clear understanding of the boundaries within which choices are permissible.

- Children benefit from situations that challenge them to work at the edge of their developing capacities and from ample opportunities to practice newly acquired skills and to acquire the disposition to persist.

- Children benefit from opportunities to collaborate with their peers and acquire a sense of being part of a community and from being treated as individuals with their own strengths, interests, and needs.

- Children need to develop a positive sense of their own self-identity and respect for other people whose perspectives and experiences may be different from their own.

- Children have enormous capacities to learn and almost boundless curiosity about the world, and they have recognized age-related limits on their cognitive and linguistic capacities.

- Children benefit from engaging in self-initiated, spontaneous play and from teacher-planned and -structured activities, projects, and experiences.

The above list is not exhaustive. Many more examples could be cited to convey the interrelationships among the principles of child development and learning or among the guidelines for early childhood practice.

Policies Essential for Achieving Developmentally Appropriate Early Childhood Programs

Early childhood professionals working in diverse situations with varying levels of funding and resources are responsible for implementing practices that are developmentally appropriate for the children they serve. Regardless of the resources available, professionals have an ethical responsibility to practice, to the best of their ability, according to the standards of their profession. Nevertheless, the kinds of practices advocated in this position statement are more likely to be implemented within an infrastructure of supportive policies and resources. NAEYC strongly recommends that policy-making groups at the state and local levels consider the following when implementing early childhood programs:

1. A comprehensive professional preparation and development system is in place to ensure that early childhood programs are staffed with qualified personnel (NAEYC 1994).

   - A system exists for early childhood professionals to acquire the knowledge and practical skills needed to practice through college-level specialized preparation in early childhood education/child development.

   - Teachers in early childhood programs are encouraged and supported to obtain and maintain, through study and participation in in-service training, current knowledge of child development and learning and its application to early childhood practice.

   - Specialists in early childhood special education are available to provide assistance and consultation in meeting the individual needs of children in the program.

   - In addition to management and supervision skills, administrators of early childhood programs have appropriate professional qualifications, including training specific to the education and development of young children, and they provide teachers time and opportunities to work collaboratively with colleagues and parents.

2. Funding is provided to ensure adequate staffing of early childhood programs and fair staff compensation that promotes continuity of relationships among adults and children (Willer 1990).

   • Funding is adequate to limit the size of the groups and provide sufficient numbers of adults to ensure individualized and appropriate care and education. Even the most well-qualified teacher cannot individualize instruction and adequately supervise too large a group of young children. An acceptable adult–child ratio for four- and five-year-olds is two adults with no more than 20 children (Ruopp, Travers, Glantz, & Coelen 1979; Francis & Self 1982; Howes 1983; Taylor & Taylor 1989; Howes, Phillips, & Whitebook 1992; Cost, Quality, & Child Outcomes Study Team 1995; Howes, Smith, & Galinsky 1995). Younger children require much smaller groups. Group size and ratio of children to adults should increase gradually through the primary grades, but one teacher with no more than 18 children or two adults with no more than 25 children is optimum (Nye, Boyd-Zaharias, Fulton, & Wallenhorst 1992; Nye, Boyd-Zaharias, & Fulton 1994). Inclusion of children with disabilities may necessitate additional adults or smaller group size to ensure that all children's needs are met.

   • Programs offer staff salaries and benefits commensurate with the skills and qualifications required for specific roles to ensure the provision of quality services and the effective recruitment and retention of qualified, competent staff. (See *Compensation Guidelines for Early Childhood Professionals* [NAEYC 1993]).

   • Decisions related to how programs are staffed and how children are grouped result in increased opportunities for children to experience continuity of relationships with teachers and other children. Such strategies include but are not limited to multiage grouping and multiyear teacher–child relationships (Katz, Evangelou, & Hartman 1990; Zero to Three 1995; Burke 1996).

3. Resources and expertise are available to provide safe, stimulating learning environments with a sufficient number and variety of appropriate materials and equipment for the

age group served (Bronson 1995; Kendrick, Kaufmann, & Messenger 1995).

4. Adequate systems for regulating and monitoring the quality of early childhood programs are in place (see position on licensing [NAEYC 1987]; accreditation criteria and procedures [NAEYC 1991]).

5. Community resources are available and used to support the comprehensive needs of children and families (Kagan 1991; NASBE 1991; Kagan, Goffin, Golub, & Pritchard 1995; NCSL 1995).

6. When individual children do not make expected learning progress, neither grade retention nor social promotion are used; instead, initiatives such as more focused time, individualized instruction, tutoring, or other individual strategies are used to accelerate children's learning (Shepard & Smith 1989; Ross, Smith, Casey, & Slavin 1995).

7. Early childhood programs use multiple indicators of progress in all development domains to evaluate the effect of the program on children's development and learning and regularly report children's progress to parents. Group-administered, standardized, multiple-choice achievement tests are not used before third grade, preferably before fourth grade. When such tests are used to demonstrate public accountability, a sampling method is used (see Shepard 1994).

REFERENCES

Adams, G., & Sandfort, J. (1994). First steps, promising futures: State prekindergarten initiatives in the early 1990s. Washington, DC: Children's Defense Fund.

Alexander, K. L., & Entwisle, D. R. (1988). *Achievement in the first 2 years of school: Patterns and processes.* Monographs of the Society for Research in Child Development (vol. 53, no. 2, serial no. 218). Ann Arbor: University of Michigan.

Arnett, J. (1989). Caregivers in day-care centers: Does training matter? *Journal of Applied Developmental Psychology, 10* (4), 541–52.

Asher, S., Hymel, S., & Renshaw, P. (1984). Loneliness in children. *Child Development, 55,* 1456–64.

Barnett, W. S. (1995). Long-term effects of early childhood programs on cognitive and school outcomes. *The Future of Children,* 5(3), 25–50.

Bergen, D. (1988). *Play as a medium for learning and development.* Portsmouth, NH: Heinemann.

Berk, L. E. (1996). *Infants and children: Prenatal through middle childhood* (2d ed.). Needham Heights, MA: Allyn & Bacon.

Berk, L., & Winsler, A. (1995). *Scaffolding children's learning: Vygotsky and early childhood education.* Washington, DC: NAEYC.

Berruetta-Clement, J. R., Schweinhart, L. J., Barnett, W. S., Epstein, A. S., & Weikart, D. P. (1984). *Changed lives: The effects of the Perry Preschool Program on youths through age 19.* Monographs of the High/Scope Educational Research Foundation (no. 8). Ypsilanti, MI: High/Scope Press.

Bodrova, E., & Leong, D. (1996). *Tools of the mind: The Vygotskian approach to early childhood education.* Englewood Cliffs, NJ: Merrill/Prentice Hall.

Bowlby, J. (1969). *Attachment and loss: Vol. 1. Attachment.* New York: Basic.

Bowman, B. (1994). The challenge of diversity. *Phi Delta Kappan, 76* (3), 218–25.

Bowman, B., & Stott, F. (1994). Understanding development in a cultural context: The challenge for teachers. In B. Mallory & R. New (Eds.), *Diversity and developmentally appropriate practices: Challenges for early childhood education.* (pp. 119–34). New York: Teachers College Press.

Bredekamp, S. (Ed.). (1987). *Developmentally appropriate practice in early childhood programs serving children from birth through age 8* (Exp. ed.). Washington, DC: NAEYC.

Bredekamp, S. (1993a). Reflections on Reggio Emilia. *Young Children, 49* (1), 13–17.

Bredekamp, S. (1993b). The relationship between early childhood education and early childhood special education: Healthy marriage or family feud? *Topics in Early Childhood Special Education, 13* (3), 258–73.

Bredekamp, S., & Rosegrant, T. (Eds.). (1992). *Reaching potentials: Appropriate curriculum and assessment for young children* (Vol. 1). Washington, DC: NAEYC.

Bredekamp, S., & Rosegrant, T. (Eds.). (1995). *Reaching potentials: Transforming early childhood curriculum and assessment* (Vol. 2). Washington, DC: NAEYC.

Bronfenbrenner, U. (1979). *The ecology of human development: Experiments by nature and design.* Cambridge, MA: Harvard University Press.

Bronfenbrenner, U. (1989). Ecological systems theory. In R. Vasta (Ed.), *Annals of child development* (Vol. 6, pp. 187–251). Greenwich, CT: JAI Press.

Bronfenbrenner, U. (1993). The ecology of cognitive development: Research models and fugitive findings. In R. H. Wozniak & K. W. Fischer (Eds.), *Development in context* (pp. 3–44). Hillsdale, NJ: Erlbaum.

Bronson, M. B. (1995). *The right stuff for children birth to 8: Selecting play materials to support development.* Washington, DC: NAEYC.

Brophy, J. (1992). Probing the subtleties of subject matter teaching. *Educational Leadership, 49* (7), 4–8.

Bruner, J. S. (1983). *Child's talk: Learning to use language.* New York: Norton.

Bruner, J. S. (1996). *The culture of education.* Cambridge, MA: Harvard University Press.

Bryant, D. M., Clifford, R., & Peisner, E. S. (1991). Best practices for beginners: Developmental appropriateness in kindergarten. *American Educational Research Journal, 28* (4), 783–803.

Burchinal, M., Robert, J., Nabo, L., & Bryant, D. (1996). Quality of center child care and infant cognitive and language development. *Child Development, 67* (2), 606–20.

Burke, D. (1996). Multi-year teacher/student relationships are a long overdue arrangement. *Phi Delta Kappan, 77* (5), 360–61.

Caine, R., & Caine, G. (1991). *Making connections: Teaching and the human brain.* New York: Addison-Wesley.

Campbell, F., & Ramey, C. (1995). Cognitive and school outcomes for high-risk African-American students at middle adolescence: Positive effects of early intervention. *American Educational Research Journal, 32* (4), 743–72.

Carnegie Task Force on Learning in the Primary Grades. (1996). *Years of promise: A comprehensive learning strategy for America's children.* New York: Carnegie Corporation of New York.

Carta, J., Schwartz, I., Atwater, J., & McConnell, S. (1991). Developmentally appropriate practice: Appraising its usefulness for young children with disabilities. *Topics in Early Childhood Special Education, 11* (1), 1–20.

Case, R., & Okamoto, Y. (1996). *The role of central conceptual structures in the development of children's thought.* Monographs of the Society of Research in Child Development (vol. 61, no. 2, serial no. 246). Chicago: University of Chicago Press.

Charlesworth, R., Hart, C. H., Burts, D. C., & DeWolf, M. (1993). The LSU studies: Building a research base for developmentally appropriate practice. In S. Reifel (Ed.), *Perspectives on developmentally appropriate practice* (Vol. 5 of *Advances in early education and day care,* pp. 3–28). Greenwich, CT: JAI Press.

Chugani, H., Phelps, M. E., & Mazziotta, J. C. (1987). Positron emission tomography study of human brain functional development. *Annals of Neurology, 22* (4), 495.

Cohen, N., & Modigliani, K. (1994). The family-to-family project: Developing family child care providers. In J. Johnson & J. B. McCracken (Eds.), *The early childhood career lattice: Perspectives on professional development* (pp. 106–10). Washington, DC: NAEYC.

Copple, C., Sigel, I. E., & Saunders, R. (1984). *Educating the young thinker: Classroom strategies for cognitive growth.* Hillsdale, NJ: Erlbaum.

Cost, Quality, & Child Outcomes Study Team. (1995). *Cost, quality, and child outcomes in child care centers, public report* (2d ed.). Denver: Economics Department, University of Colorado at Denver.

Dana Alliance for Brain Initiatives. (1996). *Delivering results: A progress report on brain research.* Washington, DC: Author.

DEC (Division for Early Childhood) Task Force on Recommended Practices. (1993). *DEC recommended practices: Indicators of quality in programs for infants and young children with special needs and their families.* Reston, VA: Council for Exceptional Children.

DEC/CEC (Division for Early Childhood of the Council for Exceptional Children). (1994). Position on inclusion. *Young Children, 49* (5), 78.

DEC/CEC & NAEYC (Division for Early Childhood of the Council for Exceptional Children & the National Association for the Education of Young Children. (1993). *Understanding the ADA—The Americans with Disabilities Act: Information for early childhood programs.* Pittsburgh, PA, & Washington, DC: Authors.

DeVries, R., & Kohlberg, W. (1990). *Constructivist early education: Overview and comparison with other programs.* Washington, DC: NAEYC.

Dewey, J. (1916). *Democracy and education: An introduction to the philosophy of education.* New York: Macmillan.

Durkin, D. (1987). A classroom-observation study of reading instruction in kindergarten. *Early Childhood Research Quarterly, 2* (3), 275–300.

Durkin, D. (1990). Reading instruction in kindergarten: A look at some issues through the lens of new basal reader materials. *Early Children Research Quarterly, 5* (3), 299–316.

Dweck, C. (1986). Motivational processes affecting learning. *American Psychologist, 41,* 1030–48.

Dyson, A. H., & Genishi, C. (1993). Visions of children as language users: Language and language education in early childhood. In B. Spodek (Ed.), *Handbook of research on the education of young children* (pp. 122–36). New York: Macmillan.

Edwards, C. P., & Gandini, L. (1989). Teachers' expectations about the timing of developmental skills: A cross-cultural study. *Young Children, 44* (4), 15–19.

Edwards, C., Gandini, L., & Forman, G. (Eds.). (1993). *The hundred languages of children: The Reggio Emilia approach to early childhood education.* Norwood, NJ: Ablex.

Erikson, E. (1963). *Childhood and society.* New York: Norton.

Feeney, S., & Kipnis, K. (1992). *Code of ethical conduct & statement of commitment.* Washington, DC: NAEYC.

Fein, G. (1981). Pretend play: An integrative review. *Child Development, 52,* 1095–118.

Fein, G., & Rivkin, M. (Eds.). (1986). *The young child at play: Reviews of research.* Washington, DC: NAEYC.

Fenson, L., Dale, P., Reznick, J. S., Bates, E., Thal, D., & Pethick, S. (1994). *Variability in early communicative development.* Monographs of the Society for Research in Child Development (vol. 59, no. 2, serial no. 242). Chicago: University of Chicago Press.

Fernald, A. (1992). Human maternal vocalizations to infants as biologically relevant signals: An evolutionary perspective. In J. H. Barkow, L. Cosmides, & J. Tooby (Eds.), *The adapted mind: Evolutionary psychology and the generation of culture* (pp. 391–428). New York: Oxford University Press.

Fields, T., Masi, W., Goldstein, S., Perry, S., & Parl, S. (1988). Infant day care facilities preschool social behavior. *Early Childhood Research Quarterly, 3* (4), 341–59.

Forman, E. A., Minick, N., & Stone, C. A. (1993). *Contexts for learning: Sociocultural dynamics in children's development.* New York: Oxford University Press.

Forman, G. (1994). Different media, different languages. In L. Katz & B. Cesarone (Eds.), *Reflections on the Reggio Emilia approach* (pp. 37–46). Urbana, IL: ERIC Clearinghouse on EECE.

Francis, P., & Self, P. (1982). Imitative responsiveness of young children in day care and home settings: The importance of the child to caregiver ratio. *Child Study Journal, 12,* 119–26.

Frede, E. (1995). The role of program quality in producing early childhood program benefits. *The Future of Children, 5* (3), 115–32.

Frede, E., & Barnett, W. S. (1992). Developmentally appropriate public school preschool: A study of implementation of the High/Scope curriculum and its effects on disadvantaged children's skills at first grade. *Early Childhood Research Quarterly, 7* (4), 483–99.

Fromberg, D. (1992). Play. In C. Seefeldt (Ed.), *The early childhood curriculum: A review of current research* (2d ed., pp. 35–74). New York: Teachers College Press.

Galinsky, E., Howes, C., Kontos, S., & Shinn, M. (1994). *The study of children in family child care and relative care: Highlights of findings.* New York: Families and Work Institute.

Gallahue, D. (1993). Motor development and movement skill acquisition in early childhood education. In B. Spodek (Ed.), *Handbook of research on the education of young children* (pp. 24–41). New York: Macmillan.

Gallahue, D. (1995). Transforming physical education curriculum. In S. Bredekamp & T. Rosegrant (Eds.), *Reaching potentials: Transforming early childhood curriculum and assessment* (Vol. 2, pp. 125–44). Washington, DC: NAEYC.

Garbarino, J., Dubrow, N., Kostelny, K., & Pardo, C. (1992). *Children in danger: Coping with the consequences of community violence.* San Francisco: Jossey-Bass.

Gardner, H. (1983). *Frames of mind: The theory of multiple intelligences.* New York: Basic.

––––––. (1991). *The unschooled mind: How children think and how schools should teach.* New York: Basic.

Gelman, R., & Baillargeon, R. (1983). A review of some Piagetian concepts. In P. H. Mussen (Ed.), *Handbook of Child Psychology* (Vol. 3, pp. 167–230). New York: Wiley.

Gelman, R., & Meck, E. (1983). Preschoolers' counting: Principles before skill. *Cognition, 13,* 343–59.

Hale-Benson, J. (1986). *Black children: Their roots, cultures, and learning styles* (Rev. ed.). Baltimore: Johns Hopkins University Press.

Herron, R., & Sutton-Smith, B. (1971). *Child's play.* New York: Wiley.

Hiebert, E. H., & Papierz, J. M. (1990). The emergent literacy construct and kindergarten and readiness books of basal reading series. *Early Childhood Research Quarterly, 5* (3), 317–34.

Hohmann, M., & Weikart, D. (1995). *Educating young children: Active learning practices for preschool and child care programs.* Ypsilanti, MI: High/Scope Educational Research Foundation.

Hollestelle, K. (1993). At the core: Entrepreneurial skills for family child care providers. In J. Johnson & J.B. McCracken (Eds.), *The early childhood career lattice: Perspectives on professional development* (pp. 63–65). Washington, DC: NAEYC.

Howes, C. (1983). Caregiver behavior in center and family day care. *Journal of Applied Developmental Psychology, 4,* 96– 107.

––––––. 1988. Relations between early child care and schooling. *Developmental Psychology, 24* (1), 53–57.

Howes, C., Phillips, D. A., & Whitebook, M. (1992). Thresholds of quality: Implications for the social development of children in center-based child care. *Child Development, 63* (2), 449–60.

Howes, C., Smith, E., & Galinsky, E. (1995). *The Florida child care quality improvement study.* New York: Families and Work Institute.

Kagan, S. L. (1991). *United we stand: Collaboration for child care and early education services.* New York: Teachers College Press.

Kagan, S., Goffin, S., Golub, S., & Pritchard, E. 1995. *Toward systematic reform: Service integration for young children and their families.* Falls Church, VA: National Center for Service Integration.

Kamii, C., & Ewing, J. K. (1996). Basing teaching on Piaget's constructivism. *Childhood Education, 72* (5), 260–64.

Katz, L. (1995). *Talks with teachers of young children: A collection.* Norwood, NJ: Ablex.

Katz, L., & Chard, S. (1989). *Engaging children minds: The project approach.* Norwood, NJ: Ablex.

Katz, L., Evangelou, D., & Hartman, J. (1990). *The case for mixed-age grouping in early education.* Washington, DC: NAEYC.

Kendrick, A., Kaufmann, R., & Messenger, K. (Eds.). (1995). *Healthy young children: A manual for programs.* Washington, DC: NAEYC.

Kohn, A. (1993). *Punished by rewards.* Boston: Houghton Mifflin.

Kostelnik, M., Soderman, A., & Whiren, A. (1993). *Developmentally appropriate programs in early childhood education.* New York: Macmillan.

Kuhl, P. (1994). Learning and representation in speech and language. *Current Opinion in Neurobiology, 4,* 812–22.

Lary, R. T. (1990). Successful students. *Education Issues, 3* (2), 11–17.

Layzer, J. I., Goodson, B. D., & Moss, M. (1993). *Life in preschool: Volume one of an observational study of early childhood programs for disadvantaged four-year-olds.* Cambridge, MA: ABT Association.

Lazar, I., & Darlington, R. (1982). *Lasting effects of early education: A report from the consortium for longitudinal studies.* Monographs of the Society for Research in Child Development (vol. 47, nos. 2–3, serial no. 195). Chicago: University of Chicago Press.

Lee, V. E., Brooks-Gunn, J., & Schuur, E. (1988). Does Head Start work? A 1-year follow-up comparison of disadvantaged children attending Head Start, no preschool, and other preschool programs. *Developmental Psychology, 24* (2), 210–22.

Legters, N., & Slavin, R. E. (1992). Elementary students at risk: A status report. Paper commissioned by the Carnegie Corporation of New York for meeting on elementary-school reform. 1–2 June.

Levy, A. K., Schaefer, L., & Phelps, P. C. (1986). Increasing preschool effectiveness: Enhancing the language abilities of 3- and 4-year-old children through planned sociodramatic play. *Early Childhood Research Quarterly, 1* (2), 133–40.

Levy, A. K., Wolfgang, C. H., & Koorland, M. A. (1992). Sociodramatic play as a method for enhancing the language performance of kindergarten age students. *Early Childhood Research Quarterly, 7* (2), 245–62.

Malaguzzi, L. (1993). History, ideas, and basic philosophy. In C. Edwards, L. Gandini, & G. Forman (Eds.), *The hundred languages of children: The Reggio Emilia approach to early childhood education* (pp. 41–89). Norwood, NJ: Ablex.

Mallory, B. (1992). Is it always appropriate to be developmental? Convergent models for early intervention practice. *Topics in Early Childhood Special Education, 11* (4), 1–12.

Mallory, B. (1994). Inclusive policy, practice, and theory for young children with developmental differences. In B. Mallory & R. New (Eds.), *Diversity and developmentally appropriate practices: Challenges for early childhood education* (pp. 44–61). New York: Teachers College Press.

Mallory, B. L., & New, R. S. (1994a). *Diversity and developmentally appropriate practices: Challenges for early childhood education.* New York: Teachers College Press.

————. (1994b). Social constructivist theory and principles of inclusion: Challenges for early childhood special education. *Journal of Special Education, 28* (3), 322–37.

Marcon, R. A. (1992). Differential effects of three preschool models on inner-city 4-year-olds. *Early Childhood Research Quarterly, 7* (4), 517–30.

Maslow, A. (1954). *Motivation and personality.* New York: Harper & Row.

Miller, L. B., & Bizzell, R. P. (1984). Long-term effects of four preschool programs: Ninth and tenth-grade results. *Child Development, 55* (4), 1570–87.

Mitchell, A., Seligson, M., & Marx, F. (1989). *Early childhood programs and the public schools.* Dover, MA: Auburn House.

Morrow, L. M. (1990). Preparing the classroom environment to promote literacy during play. *Early Childhood Research Quarterly, 5* (4), 537–54.

NAEYC. (1987). *NAEYC position statement on licensing and other forms of regulation of early childhood programs in centers and family day care.* Washington, DC: Author.

————. (1991). *Accreditation criteria and procedures of the National Academy of Early Childhood Programs* (Rev. ed.). Washington, DC: Author.

————. (1993). *Compensation guidelines for early childhood professionals.* Washington, DC: Author.

————. (1994). NAEYC position statement: A conceptual framework for early childhood professional development, adopted November 1993. *Young Children, 49* (3), 68–77.

————. (1996a). NAEYC position statement: Responding to linguistic and cultural diversity—Recommendations for effective early childhood education. *Young Children, 51* (2), 4–12.

————. (1996b). NAEYC position statement: Technology and young children—Ages three through eight. *Young Children, 51* (6), 11–16.

NAEYC & NAECS/SDE (National Association of Early Childhood Specialists in State Departments of Education). (1992). Guidelines for appropriate curriculum content and assessment in programs serving children ages 3 through 8. In S. Bredekamp & T. Rosegrant (Eds.), *Reaching potentials: Appropriate curriculum and assessment for young children* (Vol. 1, pp. 9–27). Washington, DC: NAEYC.

NASBE (National Association of State Boards of Education). (1991). *Caring communities: Supporting young children and families.* Alexandria, VA: Author.

Natriello, G., McDill, E., & Pallas, A. (1990). *Schooling disadvantaged children: Racing against catastrophe.* New York: Teachers College Press.

NCES (National Center for Education Statistics). (1993). *The condition of education, 1993.* Washington, DC: U.S. Department of Education.

NCSL (National Conference of State Legislatures). (1995). *Early childhood care and education: An investment that works.* Denver: Author.

NEGP (National Education Goals Panel). (1991). *National education goals report: Building a nation of learners.* Washington, DC: Author.

New, R. (1993). Cultural variations on developmentally appropriate practice: Challenges to theory and practice. In C. Edwards, L. Gandini, & G. Forman (Eds.), *The hundred languages of children: The Reggio Emilia approach to early childhood education* (pp. 215–32). Norwood, NJ: Ablex.

————. (1994). Culture, child development, and developmentally appropriate practices: Teachers as collaborative researchers. In B. Mallory & R. New (Eds.), *Diversity and developmentally appropriate practices: Challenges for early childhood education* (pp. 65–83). New York: Teachers College Press.

Nye, B. A., Boyd-Zaharias, J., & Fulton, B. D. (1994). *The lasting benefits study: A continuing analysis of the effect of small class size in kindergarten through third grade on student achievement test scores in subsequent grade levels— seventh grade (1992–93), technical report.* Nashville: Center of Excellence for Research in Basic Skills, Tennessee State University.

Nye, B. A., Boyd-Zaharias, J., Fulton, B. D., & Wallenhorst, M. P. (1992). Smaller classes really are better. *The American School Board Journal, 179* (5), 31–33.

Parker, J. G., & Asher, S. R. (1987). Peer relations and later personal adjustment: Are low-accepted children at risk? *Psychology Bulletin, 102* (3), 357–89.

Phillips, C. B. (1994). The movement of African-American children through sociocultural contexts: A case of conflict resolution. In B. Mallory & R. New (Eds.), *Diversity and developmentally appropriate practices: Challenges for early childhood education* (pp. 137–54). New York: Teachers College Press.

Phillips, D. A., McCartney, K., & Scarr, S. (1987). Child care quality and children's social development. *Developmental Psychology, 23* (4), 537–43.

Piaget, J. (1952). *The origins of intelligence in children.* New York: International Universities Press.

Plomin, R. (1994a). *Genetics and experience: The interplay between nature and nurture.* Thousand Oaks, CA: Sage.

————. (1994b). Nature, nurture, and social development. *Social Development, 3,* 37–53.

Powell, D. (1994). Parents, pluralism, and the NAEYC statement on developmentally appropriate practice. In B. Mallory & R. New (Eds.), *Diversity and developmentally appropriate practices: Challenges for early childhood education* (pp. 166–82). New York: Teachers College Press.

Pramling, I. (1991). Learning about "the shop": An approach to learning in preschool. *Early Children Research Quarterly, 6* (2), 151–66.

Resnick, L. (1996). Schooling and the workplace: What relationship? In *Preparing youth for the 21st century* (pp. 21–27). Washington, DC: Aspen Institute.

Rogoff, B. (1990). *Apprenticeship in thinking: Cognitive development in social context.* New York: Oxford University Press.

Rogoff, B., Mistry, J., Goncu, A., & Mosier, C. (1993). *Guided participation in cultural activity by toddlers and caregivers.* Monographs of the Society for Research in Child Development (vol. 58, no. 8, serial no. 236). Chicago: University of Chicago Press.

Ross, S. M., Smith, L. J., Casey, J., & Slavin, R. E. (1995). Increasing the academic success of disadvantaged children: An examination of alternative early intervention programs. *American Educational Research Journal, 32* (4), 773–800.

Ruopp, R., Travers, J., Glantz, F., & Coelen, C. (1979). *Children at the center: Final report of the National Day Care Study.* Cambridge, MA: ABT Associates.

Sameroff, A., & McDonough, S. (1994). Educational implications of developmental transitions: Revisiting the 5- to 7-year shift. *Phi Delta Kappan, 76* (3), 188–93.

Scarr, S., & McCartney, K. (1983). How people make their own environments: A theory of genotype—environment effects. *Child Development, 54,* 425–35.

Schrader, C. T. (1989). Written language use within the context of young children's symbolic play. *Early Childhood Research Quarterly, 4* (2), 225–44.

———. 1990. Symbolic play as a curricular tool for early literacy development. *Early Childhood Research Quarterly, 5* (1), 79–103.

Schweinhart, L. J., & Weikart, D. P. (1996). *Lasting differences: The High/Scope preschool curriculum comparison study through age 23.*

Monographs of the High/Scope Educational Research Foundation (no 12). Ypsilanti, MI: High/Scope Press.

Schweinhart, L. J., Barnes, H. V., & Weikart, D. P. (1993). *Significant benefits: The High/Scope Perry Preschool Study through age 27.* Monographs of the High/Scope Educational Research Foundation (no. 10). Ypsilanti, MI: High/Scope Press.

Schweinhart, L. J., Weikart, D. P., & Larner, M. B. (1986). Child-initiated activities in early childhood programs may help prevent delinquency. *Early Childhood Research Quarterly, 1*(3), 303–12.

Seefeldt, C. (Ed.). (1992). *The early childhood curriculum: A review of current research* (2nd ed.). New York: Teachers College Press.

Seifert, K. (1993). Cognitive development and early childhood education. In B. Spodek (Ed.), *Handbook of research on the education of young children* (pp. 9–23). New York: Macmillan.

Seppanen, P. S., Kaplan deVries, D., & Seligson, M. (1993). *National study of before and after school programs.* Portsmouth, NH: RMC Research Corp.

Shepard, L. (1994). The challenges of assessing young children appropriately. *Phi Delta Kappan, 76* (3), 206–13.

Shepard, L. A., & Smith, M. L. (1988). Escalating academic demand in kindergarten: Some nonsolutions. *Elementary School Journal, 89* (2), 135–46.

―――. (1989). *Flunking grades: Research and policies on retention.* Bristol, PA: Taylor & Francis.

Slavin, R., Karweit, N., & Madden, N. (Eds.). (1989). *Effective programs for students at-risk.* Boston: Allyn & Bacon.

Smilansky, S., & Shefatya, L. (1990). *Facilitating play: A medium for promoting cognitive, socioemotional, and academic development in young children.* Gaithersburg, MD: Psychosocial & Educational Publications.

Spodek, B. (Ed.). (1993). *Handbook of research on the education of young children.* New York: Macmillan.

Sroufe, L. A., Cooper, R. G., & DeHart, G. B. (1992). *Child development: Its nature and course* (2d ed.). New York: Knopf.

Stern, D. (1985). *The psychological world of the human infant.* New York: Basic.

Stremmel, A. J., & Fu, V. R. (1993). Teaching in the zone of proximal development: Implications for responsive teaching practice. *Child and Youth Care Forum, 22* (5), 337–50.

Taylor, J. M., & Taylor, W. S. (1989). *Communicable diseases and young children in group settings.* Boston: Little, Brown.

Tobin, J., Wu, D., & Davidson, D. (1989). *Preschool in three cultures.* New Haven, CT: Yale University Press.

U.S. Department of Health & Human Services. (1996). *Head Start performance standards.* Washington, DC: Author.

Vandell, D. L., & Corasanti, M. A. (1990). Variations in early child care: Do they predict subsequent social, emotional, and cognitive differences? *Early Childhood Research Quarterly, 5* (4), 555–72.

Vandell, D. L., & Powers, C. D. (1983). Day care quality and children's free play activities. *American Journal of Orthopsychiatry, 53* (4), 493–500.

Vandell, D. L., Henderson, V. K., & Wilson, K. S. (1988). A longitudinal study of children with day-care experiences of varying quality. *Child Development, 59* (5), 1286–92.

Vygotsky, L. (1978). *Mind in society: The development of higher psychological processes.* Cambridge, MA: Harvard University Press.

Wardle, F. (1996). Proposal: An anti-bias and ecological model for multicultural education. *Childhood Education, 72* (3), 152–56.

Wertsch, J. (1985). *Culture, communication, and cognition: Vygotskian perspectives.* New York: Cambridge University Press.

White, S. H. (1965). Evidence for a hierarchical arrangement of learning processes. In L. P. Lipsitt & C. C. Spiker (Eds.), *Advances in child development and behavior* (pp. 187–220). New York: Academic Press.

Whitebook, M., Howes, C., & Phillips, D. (1989). *The national child care staffing study: Who cares? Child care teachers and the quality of care in America.* Final report. Oakland, CA: Child Care Employee Project.

Wieder, S., & Greenspan, S. I. (1993). The emotional basis of learning. In B. Spodek (Ed.), *Handbook of research on the education of young children* (pp. 77–104). New York: Macmillan.

Willer, B. (1990). *Reaching the full cost of quality in early childhood programs.* Washington, DC: NAEYC.

Willer, B., Hofferth, S. L., Kisker, E. E., Divine-Hawkins, P., Farquhar, E., & Glantz, F. B. (1991). *The demand and supply of child care in 1990*. Washington, DC: NAEYC.

Witkin, H. (1962). *Psychological differentiation: Studies of development*. New York: Wiley.

Wolery, M., & Wilbers, J. (Eds.). (1994). *Including children with special needs in early childhood programs*. Washington, DC: NAEYC.

Wolery, M., Strain, P., & Bailey, D. (1992). Reaching potentials of children with special needs. In S. Bredekamp & T. Rosegrant (Eds.), *Reaching Potentials: Appropriate curriculum and assessment for young children* (Vol. 1, pp. 92–111). Washington, DC: NAEYC.

Zero to Three: The National Center. (1995). *Caring for infants and toddlers in groups: Developmentally appropriate practice*. Arlington, VA: Author.

GUIDELINES FOR DEVELOPMENTALLY APPROPRIATE PRACTICE

NAEYC's DAP guidelines can be implemented in your daily work with children:

Create a caring environment among children and adults
Children:
- learn personal responsibility
- develop constructive relationships with others
- respect individual and cultural difference

Adults:
- get to know each child, taking into account individual differences and developmental level
- adjust the pace and content of the curriculum so that children can be successful most of the time
- bring each child's culture and language into the setting, welcoming their families
- expect children to be tolerant of others' differences

The curriculum and schedule allow children to select and initiate their own activities
Children:
- learn through active involvement in a variety of learning experiences
- build independence by taking on increasing responsibilities
- initiate their own activities to follow their interests

Adults:
- provide a variety of materials and activities that are concrete and real
- provide a variety of work places and spaces
- arrange the environment so that children can work alone or in groups

- extend children's learning by posing problems, asking thought-provoking questions
- add complexity to tasks as needed
- model, demonstrate, and provide information so children can progress in their learning

The program is organized and integrated so that children develop a deeper understanding of key concepts and skills
Children:
- engage in activities that reflect their current interests
- plan and predict outcomes of their research
- share information and knowledge with others

Adults:
- plan related activities and experiences that broaden children's knowledge and skills
- design curriculum to foster important skills like literacy and numeracy
- adapt instruction for children who are ahead or behind age-appropriate expectations
- plan curriculum so that children achieve important developmental goals

Activities and experiences help children develop a positive self-image within a democratic community
Children:
- learn through reading books about other cultures
- read about current events and discuss how these relate to different cultures
- accept differences among their peers, including children with disabilities

Adults:
- provide culturally and non-sexist activities and materials that foster children's self-identity
- design the learning environment so children can learn new skills while using their native language
- allow children to demonstrate their learning using their own language
- facilitate discussion and problem solving among children

Activities and experiences develop children's awareness of the
importance of community involvement

Children:

- are ready and eager to learn about the world outside
  their immediate environment
- are open to considering different ways of thinking or
  doing things
- can benefit from contact with others outside their
  homes or child care setting

Adults:

- encourage awareness of the community at large, as
  well as a sense of the classroom community
- plan experiences in facilities within the community
- bring outside resources and volunteers into the child
  care setting
- encourage children to plan their involvement based
  on their own interests

PROFESSIONAL ORGANIZATIONS

When looking to further your development, a professional organization is a great place to start. There are several organizations, some of which even have state or local affiliates.

National Association for the Education of Young Children (NAEYC)

1509 16th Street, NW
Washington DC 20036
800-424-2460
www.naeyc.org
E-mail membership@naeyc.org

Specific membership benefits:

Comprehensive members receive all the benefits of regular membership described below plus annually receive five or six books immediately after their release by NAEYC.

Regular and student members receive:

- Six issues of *Young Children,* which includes timely articles on pertinent issues, as well as suggestions and strategies for enhancing children's learning
- Reduced registration fees at NAEYC-sponsored local and national conferences and seminars
- Discounted prices on hundreds of books, videos, brochures and posters from NAEYC's extensive catalog of materials
- Access to the *Members Only* Web site, including links to additional resources and chat sites for communication with other professionals

National Association of Child Care Professionals (NACCP)

P.O. Box 90723
Austin, TX 78709
800-537-1118
www.naccp.org

Specific membership benefits:

Management Tools of the Trade™

Your membership provides complete and FREE access (a $79 value) to these effective management tools that provide technical assistance in human resource management. In addition, members will receive NACCP's quarterly trade journals, *Professional Connections©*, *Teamwork©*, and *Caring for Your Children©*, to help you stay on top of hot issues in child care. Each edition also includes a Tool of the Trade™.

National Child Care Association (NCCA)

1016 Rosser St.
Conyers GA 30012
800-543-7161
www.nccanet.org

Specific membership benefits:
- As the only recognized voice in Washington DC, NCCA has great influence on our legislators
- Professional development opportunities are available

Association for Education International (ACEI)

The Olney Professional Building
17904 Georgia Avenue, Suite 215
Olney, MD 20832
Phone: 800-423-2563 or 301-570-2122
Fax: 301-570-2212
Web site: http://www.acei.org

ACEI is an international organization dedicated to promoting the best educational practices throughout the world.

Specific membership benefits:

- Workshops and travel/study tours abroad
- Four issues per year of the journal *Childhood Education* and the *Journal of Research in Childhood Education*
- Hundreds of resources for parents and teachers, including books, pamphlets, audiotapes, and videotapes

National AfterSchool Association (NAA)

1137 Washington Street
Boston, MA 02124
Phone: 617-298-5012
Fax: 617-298-5022
Web site: http://www.naaweb.org

NAA is a national organization dedicated to providing information, technical assistance, and resources concerning children in out-of-school programs. Members include teachers, policy makers, and administrators representing all public, private, and community-based sectors of after-school programs.

Specific member benefits:

- A subscription to the NAA journal, *School-Age Review*
- A companion membership in state affiliates
- Discounts on NAA publications and products
- Discount on NAA annual conference registration
- Opportunity to be an NAA accreditation endorser
- Public policy representatives in Washington, DC

OTHER ORGANIZATIONS TO CONTACT:

The Children's Defense Fund

25 E. St. NW
Washington DC 20001
202-628-8787
www.childrensdefense.org

National Association for Family Child Care

P.O. Box 10373
Des Moines, IA 50306
800-359-3817
www.nafcc.org
Journal: *The National Perspective*

National Black Child Development Institute

1023 15th Ave. NW
Washington DC 20002
202-833-2220
www.nbcdi.org

National Head Start Association

1651 Prince Street
Alexandria VA 22314
703-739-0875
www.nhsa.org
Journal: *Children and Families*

International Society for the Prevention of Child Abuse and Neglect

25 W. 560 Geneva Road, Suite L2C
Carol Stream, IL 60188
630-221-1311
http://www.ispcan.org
Journal: *Child Abuse and Neglect: The International Journal*

Council for Exceptional Children

1110 N. Glebe Road, Suite 300
Arlington, VA 22201
888-CEC-SPED
www.cec.sped.org
Journal: *CEC Today*

National Association for Bilingual Education

Union Center Plaza
810 First Street, NE
Washington DC 20002
www.nabe.org
Journal: *NABE Journal of Research and Practice*

International Reading Association

800 Barksdale Road
P.O. Box 8139
Newark, DE 19714
800-336-READ
www.reading.org
Journal: *The Reading Teacher*

National Education Organization (NEA)

1201 16th St. NW
Washington, DC 20036
202-833-4000
www.nea.org
Journals: *Works4Me and NEA Focus,* by online subscription.

Zero to Three: National Center for Infants, Toddlers, and Families

2000 M. Street NW, Suite 200
Washington DC 20036
202-638-1144
www.zerotothree.org
Journal: *Zero to Three*

RESOURCES

BOOKS

Baker, A., & Manfredi/Petitt, L. (2004). *Relationships. The heart of quality care: Creating community among adults in early care settings.* Washington, DC: NAEYC.

Bisson, J. (1997). *Celebrate: An anti-bias guide to enjoying holidays in early childhood programs.* Mt. Rainier, MD: Gryphon House.

Brazelton, T. B., & Greenspan, S. (2000). *The irreducible needs of children: What every child must have to grow, learn, and flourish.* Cambridge, MA: Perseus.

Canter, L. (2002). *Parents on your side: A teacher's guide to creating positive relationships with parents* (2nd ed.). Los Angeles: Canter and Associates.

Children's Defense Fund. (2005). *The state of America's children: Yearbook 2005.* Washington, DC: Author

Coontz, S. (1997). *The way we really are: Coming to terms with America's changing families.* New York: Basic Books.

Diffily, D., & Morrison, K. (Eds.). (1996). *Family-friendly communication for early childhood programs.* Washington, DC: NAEYC.

Dombro, A., O'Donnell, N., Galinsky, E., Gilkeson, S., & Farber, A. (1996). *Community mobilization: Strategies to support young children and their families.* New York: Families and Work Institute.

Epstein, J. (2000). *School and family partnerships: Preparing educators and improving schools.* Boulder, CO: Westview.

Fine, M., & Lee, S. (2000). *Handbook of diversity in parent education: The changing faces of parenting and parent education.* New York: Academic Press.

Gonzales-Mena, J. (2000). *Multicultural issues in child care* (3rd ed.). Mountain View, CA: Mayfield Publishing Co.

Hildebrand, V., Phenice, L., Gray, M., Hines, R., Bubolz, M., & Sontag, M. (1999). *Knowing and serving diverse families* (2nd ed.). Englewood Cliffs, NJ: Merrill.

Jaksek, C. (2004). *The difficult parent: An educator's guide to handling aggressive* parents. Thousand Oaks, CA: Corwin Press, a division of Sage.

Miller, K. (1996). *The crisis manual for early childhood teachers: How to handle the really difficult problems.* Beltsville, MD: Gryphon House.

Rudney, G. (2005). *Every teacher's guide to working with parents.* Thousand Oaks, CA: Corwin Press, a division of Sage.

Seligman, M. (2000). *Conducting effective conferences with parents of children with disabilities: A guide for teachers.* New York: Guilford Press.

Tabors, P. (1997). *One child, two languages: A guide for preschool educators of children learning English as a second language.* Baltimore, MD: Paul H. Brookes Publishing Co.

Teaching Tolerance. (1997). *Starting small: Teaching tolerance in preschool and the early grades.* Montgomery, AL: Southern Poverty Law Center.

Whitaker, T., & Fiore, D. (2000). *Dealing with difficult parents, and with parents in difficult situations.* Larchmont, NY: Eye on Education.

York, S. (2003). *Roots and wings: Affirming culture in early childhood programs. Rev. Ed.* St. Paul, MN: Redleaf Press.

INTERNET RESOURCES

Action Alliance for Children
http://www.4children.org
Action Alliance for Children exists to inform, educate, and persuade a statewide constituency of people who work with and on behalf of children by providing reliable information on current issues, trends, and public policies that affect children and families. AAC is a resource for policymakers, children's service providers and advocates, and the media.

Adoption Information Institute

http://www.adoptioninformationinstitute.org

This organization's mission is to enhance the understanding of adoption by educating the public about adoption. Find information here about *An Educator's Guide to Adoption.*

American Academy of Child and Adolescent Psychiatry

http://www.aacap.org

Search for Facts for Families to prove concise and up-to-date information on issues that affect children, teenagers, and their families

American Academy of Pediatrics

http://www.aap.org

The mission of the American Academy of Pediatrics is to attain optimal physical, mental, and social health and well-being for all infants, children, adolescents, and young adults. Information on this site could be useful for designing parent meetings on a variety of topics.

http://atozteacherstuff.com

This teacher-created Web site is designed to help teachers find online resources.

Children's Defense Fund

http://www.childrensdefense.org

The mission of the Children's Defense Fund is to Leave No Child Behind® and to ensure every child a Healthy Start, a Head Start, a Fair Start, a Safe Start, and a Moral Start in life and successful passage to adulthood with the help of caring families and communities. There is much information at this site about community issues to support family needs.

Council for Exceptional Children (CEC)

http://www.cec.sped.org

The worldwide mission of the Council for Exceptional Children is to improve educational outcomes for individuals with exceptionalities.

Culturally and Linguistically Appropriate Services

http://www.clas.uiuc.edu

The CLAS Institute identifies, evaluates, and promotes effective and appropriate early intervention practices and preschool practices that are sensitive and respectful to children and families from culturally and linguistically diverse backgrounds.

Family Support America

http://www.familysupportamerica.org

Family Support America, formerly Family Resource Coalition of America, promotes family support as the nationally recognized movement to strengthen and support families.

Federation for Children with Special Needs

http://www.fcsn.org

Federation for Children with Special Needs (FCSN) is a center for parents and parent organizations to work together on behalf of children with special needs and their families. FCSN is a coalition of parent groups representing children with a variety of disabilities, offering a variety of services to parents, parent groups, and others who are concerned with children with special needs.

http://www.inspiringteachers.com

This teacher-created Web site is dedicated to empowering teachers and improving student success. Click on Teacher's toolbox, then on Articles and Parent Communication to find information on using parent volunteers in the classroom.

National Association for Family Child Care

http://www.nafcc.org

The focus of NAFCC is to provide technical assistance to family child care associations. This assistance is provided through developing leadership and professionalism, addressing issues of diversity, and by promoting quality and professionalism through NAFCC's Family Child Care Association. This site has helpful information on good beginnings for children and families.

National Child Care Information Center

http://nccic.org

Many resources and links on child care and early education, and families.

National Clearinghouse on Child Abuse and Neglect Information

http://nccach.acf.hhs.gov

National Clearinghouse on Child Abuse and Neglect Information is sponsored by the Administration for Children and Families under the Department of Health and Human Services. The Clearinghouse is a national resource for professionals and others seeking information on child abuse and neglect and child welfare.

http://www.NEA.org

The Web site of the National Education Association has much information for teachers and parents. Click on Parents and Community to find an article, "How to Make Parent–Teacher Conferences Work for Your Child."

National Coalition for Parent Involvement in Education

http://www.ncpie.org

National Coalition for Parent Involvement in Education (NCPIE) is a coalition of major education, community, public service, and advocacy organizations working to create meaningful family–school partnerships in every school in America.

The National Parent Information Network

http://www.npin.org

The National Parent Information Network is sponsored by ERIC, and offers access to research and information about the process of parenting and family involvement in education.

http://teacher/scholastic.com

This Web site has many resources for teachers, including information on ways to communicate effectively with families.

Teaching Tolerance, Southern Poverty Law Center

http://www.tolerance.org

Free information for teachers on developing accepting classrooms.

Touchpoints

http://www.touchpoints.org

Touchpoints, Dr. Berry Brazelton's organization, offers training based on the work of Dr. T. Berry Brazelton, which combines relationship building and child development into a framework that professionals can use to enhance their work with families.

VIDEOS FOR CAREGIVERS

Building Bridges Between Teachers and Families by Margie Carter, Harvest Resources.

VHS. 21 minutes.

Two teachers, in very different economic and cultural settings, share a dialogue as they move from a focus on educating parents to being allies with families.

Available from Redleaf Press, 800-423-8309 www.redleafpress.org

The Child in the Family.

VHS. 24 minutes.

Roles of parents, functions of family.

Magna System Inc., 95 West County Line Road, Barrington, IL 60010, 800-523-5503.

Conducting Effective Conferences with Parents.

VHS. 22 minutes.

Insight Media, 2612 Broadway, New York, NY 10024 212-721-6316.

Cultivating Roots: Home/School Partnerships.

Part of video series *The Early Childhood Program: A Place to Learn and Grow.*

VHS. 30 minutes.

NAEYC , www.naeyc.org, 800-424-2460.

Do Children Also Divorce?

VHS. 30 minutes.

To show parents and teachers the important role they must play in meeting children's needs during a divorce.

Filmakers Library, 133 E. 58th St., New York, NY 10022, 212-808-4980, www.filmakers.com

Families and Schools: Teaming for Success.

VHS. 2 parts. 30 minutes each.

Strategies for establishing parent involvement programs, including mandates for increased parent involvement.

Insight Media, 2612 Broadway, New York, NY 10024 212-721-6316.

First Moves: Welcoming a Child to a New Caregiving Setting.

VHS. 29 minutes.

Useful information about how to get children and families off to a good start.

Child Care Video Magazine. California State Dept. of Education, Sacramento, CA, 916-445-1260.

How to Talk with Parents in the Informal Conference.

VHS. 40 minutes.

Information about communication that can be helpful to teachers of all ages.

Insight Media, 2612 Broadway, New York, NY 10024 212-721-6316.

Involving Families in Active Learning Settings.

VHS. 23 minutes.

Includes home visits with other methods, such as classroom visits.

High/Scope Educational Research Foundation, 600 West River St., Ypsilanti, MI 48197. www.highscope.org

Partnerships in Parenting.

VHS. 27 minutes.

Descriptions of two collaborative programs.

Early Childhood National Programming at South Carolina ETV, 1001 George Rogers Blvd., Columbia, SC 29201 803-737-3417.

Partnerships with Parents.

VHS. 28 minutes.

This video portrays both the benefits and some of the challenges in forming partnerships with parents.

NAEYC #857, www.naeyc.org, 800-424-2460.

Protective Urges; Working with the Feelings of Parents and Caregivers.

VHS. 27 minutes.

The program for infant–toddler caregivers.

California Dept. of Education, Bureau of Publications, 560 J St. #220, Sacramento, CA 95814, 916-445-1260.

Someday's Child: A Focus on Special Needs Children and Their Families.

VHS. 30 minutes.

Educational Productions Inc., 4925 SW Humphrey Park Crest, Portland, OR 97221, www.edpro.com, 800-950-4949.

CASE STUDY #1

Understanding Roberto's Background

Twelve-year-old Roberto has been falling behind his classmates. He does not do his homework, and he looks very tired when he is in class. He is quiet, and when the teacher asks him to tell her if he is having any problems, he refuses to answer. She has twice called his home to get his parents to come in for a conference, and each time Roberto answers the phone and says his parents are working. The teacher can hear other children crying and playing in the background. She is frustrated and feels his parents just don't care.

1. What would you do if you were this teacher?

2. What could be some factors influencing this situation?

3. What should the teacher consider, in planning an appropriate response?

Answer: Without knowing much more about the family background, it would be a mistake for this teacher to assume Roberto's parents don't care. Possible reasons for the family and Roberto's behavior: language and cultural barriers; socioeconomic conditions that put both parents at work and Roberto in charge of younger siblings; other environmental stresses.

Some strategies for the teacher:

- learn more about family from administrator, school counselor, other teachers, community resources;

- find an interpreter who can help her make contact with family, perhaps with notes in their language;

- keep on working on building relationship with Roberto;

- learn if there are community resources to link Roberto's family;

- make flexible plans for making contact with family, such as home visits;

- persist in efforts.

CASE STUDY #2

Dealing with Hostility

Ms. Downing comes to a conference with her son's second grade teacher. Soon after the teacher begins going through a skills checklist and pointing out what Jacob has accomplished and areas that need help, the parent bursts out angrily at the teacher. She says that Jacob had no problems last year, and his teacher last year was only positive. She ends by shouting, "If you were only doing your job properly, Jacob would be doing just fine."

1. How should the teacher react? How do you imagine she feels?

2. What would be unhelpful responses?

3. What would be more helpful responses?

Answer: The least appropriate response is for the teacher to lose control and get angry. Rather than taking the parent's behavior personally, the teacher's best response is to use active listening strategies, reflecting back and paraphrasing the parent's words. Indicating to the parent that the teacher is trying to understand her point of view may help defuse the situation. Get as much information as possible, write down the concerns, keep the parent talking. If the parent is still unable to calm down, it may be best for the teacher to set up another conference, perhaps inviting a neutral third party to be present.

CASE STUDY #3

Differences in Perspective on Appropriate Curriculum

Mr. Thomas has been watching the children in the preschool classroom at play. He comes to Stephanie, the lead teacher, and complains about the curriculum in the preschool, suggesting that it is "just play," and not likely to prepare his child for success in elementary school. He hints that if the curriculum does not change to more obvious learning, he is going to remove his child from the school and find a school that can better help his child learn.

1. If you were Stephanie, what might be your initial reaction?

2. What are important kinds of knowledge that Stephanie needs to draw upon in framing her response to Mr. Thomas?

3. How can Stephanie demonstrate to this parent, as well as the other parents, how play is helping children learn?

Answer: Teachers should indicate that they agree with the parent in wanting to prepare the child for school success. However, it is appropriate to provide information and explanations for the parent that indicate the genuine learning going on through the curriculum. Inviting a parent to observe frequently may provide helpful first-hand understanding of the preschool learning process. Helping parents understand readiness of the whole child is an important responsibility for teachers, and they must use repeated forms of communication to achieve this. Parents cannot be expected to understand the nature of best curricula for preschoolers without clear and repeated explanations from teachers. Printed information, meetings that use videos for the teacher to point out the real learning, are all strategies that may be helpful.

CASE STUDY #4

When Families Appear Unresponsive

Anne Morgan is very discouraged because only four parents showed up for the meeting she had organized last week. She had carefully planned a meeting on a topic she felt that all parents should understand. She tells her administrator that she is just not going to go to all that effort again, because the parents don't seem to really care enough to come out to a meeting.

1. How would Anne's attitude act as a barrier to forming partnerships with families?

2. What factors might have influenced the low attendance at the parent meeting?

3. What strategies might help future efforts attract more interest?

Answer: The worst thing she could do would be to abandon her efforts to involve parents and discontinue all future meetings. Some things she could try to improve attendance could be:

- Involve parents in helping formulate plans for future meetings, making decisions regarding best times for meetings, topics and formats that appeal, as well as other circumstances that could influence attendance.

- Continue to communicate with families in as many ways as possible, so that parents feel involved in the classroom and learning opportunities.

- Make sure that language is not a barrier, providing interpreters and translators as needed.

- Persist. Remember that it is a primary role for a teacher to work with families, and keep trying to find ways to reach them.

ISSUES AND TRENDS

CODE OF ETHICS

The Code of Ethical Conduct and Statement of Commitment, approved by NAEYC's Governing Board in 1989 and revised in 2005, includes a section of ethical responsibilities to families, articulating nine ideals and fifteen specific principles governing actions. Teachers should be familiar with the ideals and principles of the Code, in order to make appropriate decisions in their interaction with families. The ideals are:

1. To be familiar with the knowledge base related to working effectively with families and to stay informed through continuing education and training.

2. To develop relationships of mutual trust and create partnerships with the families we serve.

3. To welcome all family members and encourage them to participate in the program.

4. To listen to families, acknowledge and build upon their strengths and competencies, and learn from families as we support families in their task of nurturing children.

5. To respect the dignity and preferences of each family and to make an effort to learn about its structure, culture, language, customs, and beliefs.

6. To acknowledge families' child-rearing values and their right to make decisions for their children.

7. To share information about each child's education and development with families and to help them understand and appreciate the current knowledge base of the early childhood profession.

8. To help family members enhance their understanding of their children and support the continuing development of their skills as parents.

9. To participate in building support networks for families by providing them with opportunities to interact with program staff, other families, community resources, and professional services (Code of Ethical Conduct and Statement of Commitment, Rev. NAEYC, 2005).

The fifteen principles that are enunciated in this section of the Code are useful in helping teachers determine appropriate professional actions when faced with dilemmas in serving families.

P-2.1—We shall not deny family members access to their child's classroom or program setting unless access is denied by court order or other legal restriction.

P-2.2—We shall inform families of program philosophy, policies, curriculum, assessment system, and personnel qualifications, and explain why we teach as we do—which should be in accordance with our ethical responsibilities to children.

P-2.3—We shall inform families of and, when appropriate, involve them in policy decisions.

P-2.4—We shall involve the family in significant decisions about their child.

P-2.5—We shall make every effort to communicate effectively with all families in a language that they understand. We shall use community resources for translation and interpretation when we do not have sufficient resources in our own programs.

P-2.6—As families share information with us about their children and families, we shall consider this information to plan and implement the program.

P-2.7—We shall inform families about the nature and purpose of the program's child assessments and how data about their child will be used.

P-2.8—We shall treat child assessment information confidentially and share this information only when there is a legitimate need for it.

P-2.9—We shall inform the family of injuries and incidents involving their child, of risks such as exposures to communicable diseases that might result in infection, and of occurrences that might result in emotional stress.

P-2.10—Families shall be fully informed of any proposed research projects involving their children and shall have the opportunity to give or withhold consent without penalty. We shall not permit or participate in research that could in any way hinder the education, development, or well-being of children.

P-2.11—We shall not engage in or support exploitation of families. We shall not use our relationship with a family for private advantage or personal gain, or enter into relationships with family members that might impair our effectiveness working with their children.

P-2.12—We shall develop written policies for the protection of confidentiality and the disclosure of children's records. These policy documents shall be made available to all program personnel and families. Disclosure of children's records beyond family members, program personnel, and consultants having an obligation of confidentiality shall require familial consent (except in cases of abuse or neglect).

P-2.13—We shall maintain confidentiality and shall respect the family's right to privacy, refraining from disclosure of confidential information and intrusion into family life. However, when we have reason to believe that a child's welfare is at risk, it is permissible to share confidential information with agencies, as well as with individuals who have legal responsibility for intervening in the child's interest.

P-2.14—In cases where family members are in conflict with one another, we shall work openly, sharing our observations of the child, to help all parties involved make informed decisions. We shall refrain from becoming an advocate for one party.

P-2.15—We shall be familiar with and appropriately refer families to community resources and professional support services. After a referral has been made, we shall follow up to ensure that services have been appropriately provided.

Teachers working with children of all ages should be familiar with and bound by these ideals and principles. In addition, teachers should obtain a copy of the full Code of Ethics, which also enunciates ideals and principles related to responsibilities to children, to co-workers and employers, and to the community. Professional responsibility means making ethical decisions in the face of dilemmas that arise in the course of daily contact with other.

NO CHILD LEFT BEHIND (NCLB) LEGISLATION

The Elementary and Secondary Education Act, commonly known as No Child Left Behind, was signed into law in 2002 (PL 107-10), and has far-reaching effects on educational systems, schools, classrooms, and the children served. There are four main goals behind the law that include:

- stronger accountability for results measured by student achievement test scores, with corrective actions to be taken as needed;

- more freedom for state and communities to use federal education funds;

- encouraging the use of proven education methods to improve student learning and achievement; and

- more choices for parents.

Teachers should be familiar with all provisions of the law, but it is these choices and opportunities for families mandated by the law that we will focus on here.

Parents of children in low-performing schools have new options for making changes for their children. In schools that do not meet state standards for at least two consecutive years, parents may transfer their children to better-performing public schools, including charter schools, within their district, with transportation provided by the district. Students from low-income families that fail to meet state standards for at least three years are eligible to receive supplemental educational services, such as free tutoring, after-school services, and summer school. Parents can also choose another public school if the school their child attends is unsafe.

Schools are required to give parents an annual report card that shows how well students in each school performed, broken out by race, gender, disability, and so on, so parents can clearly see how well their school is performing. In addition, parents must be given an annual report about how teacher qualifications at the school meet the law's requirements.

In addition to these family rights, the law makes clear statements about requirements for parent involvement. The requirements include:

- a written parent involvement policy that has included parents in creating and evaluating the policy

- involvement of parents in planning, evaluating, and improving the various programs for parents

- giving parents understandable descriptions and explanations of the curricula and forms of academic assessments used to measure student progress

- offering a flexible number of meetings for parents at various times, and using funds to provide transportation, child care, and home visits to facilitate parent attendance

- emphasizing the importance of communication, including (a minimum of) annual parent–teacher conferences in each elementary school, frequent reports to parents of children's progress, reasonable access to staff, and opportunities to volunteer, participate, and observe in their children's classrooms

- building the capacity for parent involvement, including providing assistance to understand curriculum content and offer materials and training to help parents work with their children, such as with literacy training and technology

- educating teachers on how to reach out to, communicate and work with parents as equal partners, and build ties between parents and the schools

- training parents to enhance the involvement of other parents

- sharing responsibilities between home and school for high student achievement

- coordinating parent involvement activities with Head Start, Reading First, Early Reading First, Parents as Teachers, HIPPY, and public preschools to encourage parents to participate more fully

- establishing parental information and resource centers

Parental information and resource centers (PIRC) are to assist parents of children identified for improvement under Title I. These school-based and school-linked centers are designated to help implement effective parental involvement policies, programs, and activities that will improve children's academic success. Another purpose is to develop and strengthen partnerships among parents (including parents of children birth through age five), teachers, and their children's schools and programs. Fifty percent of the funds designated for PIRC are to serve areas with a high concentration of low-income families; of the funds, a minimum of 30 percent is to be used to establish, expand, or operate early childhood parent education programs. See information about the PIRC program at the Web site www.pirc.org.

With these provisions and requirements, the Act is sending clear messages to schools about the necessity of parent involvement programs in all schools. It will be important for teachers to understand the requirements of the law, and to be able to help interpret them to families. Hopefully, this begins a new era of home and school communication and partnership.

There are two resources that could be particularly useful to teachers trying to help parents understand the implications of NCLB for themselves and their children. A fact sheet, titled *Facts and Terms Every Parent Should Know,* is available to download and print from the Department of Education Web site at www.ed.gov. A booklet, *A Practical Guide for Talking with your Community about No Child Left Behind and Schools in Need of Improvement,* is available from the Learning First Alliance, see information on Web site www. learningfirst.org, and click on publications.

Educators must keep aware of how this legislation is affecting school practices that affect children, families, and teachers themselves. It is important for teachers to advocate for best practices, and endeavor to change practices that are not actually improving education. Only time will tell the effects of NCLB.

CHILD ABUSE AND NEGLECT

No matter in what community teachers work, or with what age group of children, they will encounter child abuse and neglect, as well as other aspects of family violence, and must be prepared to understand their ethical and legal obligations for action. Children may be abused physically, sexually, or emotionally, and neglect occurs when parents or caregivers do not provide essential care, even when resources are made available to them. Teachers are often among the first people to learn that a family is troubled by abuse and neglect, or by violence within the family, and therefore have special opportunities to help these families. The following are some of the indicators that teachers should consider suspicious.

Physical Abuse

There are four general groups of injuries that may result from physical abuse. These include injuries to the skin and soft under tissues, including bruises, abrasions, bites, and burns; injuries to the skeletal system from direct blows or from shaking or squeezing; injuries to the head and central nervous system from being shaken or choked; or internal injuries from being punched, kicked, or thrown.

Teachers might see:

Physical Indicators of Physical Abuse

- unexplained bruises or welts, especially in places where child's physical activity cannot account for them: on the face, throat, upper arms, buttocks, thighs, backs of knees, or lower back

- bilateral marks, or those with unusual patterns that suggest the use of an instrument (belt buckle or electrical cord)

- unexplained small burns, as made by match or cigarette, especially on palms, soles of feet, abdomen, or buttocks

- immersion burns, producing marks like socks or gloves on feet or hands, or a doughnut-shaped burn on buttocks

- rope burns

- infected burns, indicating a delay in treatment

Behavioral Indicators of Physical Abuse

- wearing inappropriate clothing to cover physical indicators

- inappropriate, excessive fear of parent or caretaker

- unbelievable, inconsistent explanations for injuries

- unusual shyness and wariness of physical contact

- extremes of behavior—withdrawal, aggression, regression, depression

- (infant) lies unusually still while surveying surroundings

Sexual Abuse

Physical Indicators of Sexual Abuse

- stained or bloody underwear
- difficulty sitting or walking
- frequent unexplained sore throats, yeast, or urinary infections
- somatic complaints, including pain and irritation of genitals
- sexually transmitted diseases or pregnancy

Behavioral Indicators of Sexual Abuse

- disclosure
- regressive behavior, such as thumb sucking, wetting, fear of dark
- disturbed sleep patterns and recurring nightmares
- unusual or age-inappropriate interest in sexual matters
- avoidance of undressing or wearing extra layers of clothing
- sudden decrease in school performance or truancy
- promiscuity or seductive behavior

Emotional Abuse

Physical Indicators of Emotional Abuse

- eating disorders—obesity or anorexia
- speech disorders—stuttering or stammering
- developmental delays in speech or motor skills
- weight or height substantially below norm
- nervous disorders—rashes, hives, tics, stomachaches
- (infants) flat or bald spots on head

Behavioral Indicators of Emotional Abuse

- habit disorders—biting, rocking, head banging
- cruel behaviors—taking apparent pleasure in hurting animals, children, adults

- age-inappropriate behaviors—wetting or soiling
- behavioral extremes—listless/excitable, overly compliant/defiant

Neglect

Physical Indicators of Neglect

- poor hygiene, including lice, scabies, severe diaper rash, body odor
- squinting
- clothing unsuitable for weather, or missing key items of clothing
- untreated injury or illness
- lack of immunizations
- height and weight significantly below age norms

Behavioral Indicators of Neglect

- unusual school attendance and absenteeism
- chronic hunger, tiredness, lethargy
- begging for food
- report of no caretaker at home

Abuse and neglect may include any or all of these indicators, and is not limited to these.

Questions Teachers Can Ask Themselves

- Does the child have a low threshold for frustration, with crying over tiny difficulties?
- Does the child's mood shift abruptly, without apparent reason?
- Do the parents appear to be hiding something? Do they deny or minimize any observable injuries, or give explanations that do not seem plausible?
- Does the child appear withdrawn, depressed, or have difficulty making friends?

- Does the child threaten or bully to get his way? Is the child timid, passive, or fearful with peers?

- Is the child apprehensive about going home? Does the child express a wish that you were his parent?

- Does the child appear sleepy or lethargic at school?

- Does child frequently have stomachaches or headaches?

- Does the child seem preoccupied, or startle easily?

Teacher's Role

When a teacher suspects abuse or neglect in a family situation, there are several courses of action indicated. Information gathering and clarifying should occur continually as teachers try to determine if there is cause for concern.

Teachers ask for explanations of injuries or appearances, neutrally inquiring, "What happened to your knee?" or "What did the doctor say about the bruises?" so that the child or parent may explain the situation without being put on the defensive. Parental responses may either confirm teacher suspicions or resolve the question. The director or principal should have an opportunity to observe the concerning injury or behavior.

Document Evidence

When teachers become aware of possible abuse and neglect, documentation of what they see must be kept. Such records indicate patterns for teachers and administrators and may determine their next actions. Documentation is to substantiate any suspicions with recorded evidence, and is useful to an investigator.

Many schools or programs will have devised their own forms for such documentation. Otherwise, simple, objective descriptions are all that is required, including the child's full name, and the date when the information was recorded, as well as the date when the observation occurred. Include also the verbatim conversations held with the child and/or the parent. If concerns are removed after clarification with the family, documentation may be the only step to take at this time.

Nov. 18th. Two large bruises, on each upper arm, including distinct finger marks.

Dec. 3rd. Bright red welts on backs of legs. Child reports father was very angry previous night.

As teachers document, they should also keep administrators informed of their concerns.

Report to Proper Agencies

Laws in all states and provinces mandate teachers and child care workers to report cases of suspected abuse. Teachers should check their own local regulations for current laws and the appropriate protective agency to whom to report. In addition to the mandate of law to report, the NAEYC Code of Ethical Conduct clearly states obligations for early childhood professionals.

Under the section regarding ethical responsibilities to children, the following principles are directly related:

P-1.5—We shall be familiar with the symptoms of child abuse, including physical, sexual, verbal, and emotional abuse, and neglect. We shall know and follow state laws and community procedures that protect children against abuse and neglect.

P-1.6—When we have reasonable cause to suspect child abuse or neglect, we shall report it to the appropriate community agency and follow up to ensure that appropriate action has been taken. When appropriate, parents or guardians will be informed that the referral has been made.

P-1.7—When another person tells us of a suspicion that a child is being abused or neglected, we shall assist that person in taking appropriate action to protect the child.

P-1.8—When a child protective agency fails to provide adequate protection for abused or neglected children, we acknowledge a collective ethical responsibility to work toward improvement of these services.

In reporting, the burden of proof is not on teachers, but on the protective services agency to whom teachers must report; if a report of suspected abuse or neglect is made in good faith (contrasted with the malicious intention of a parent who is trying to discredit another in a custody battle, for example), the reporting adult is protected from liability.

There are instances of teachers and schools who try to close their eyes to the problems they suspect or see in families, perhaps fearing reprisals or parents' anger if they involve themselves in "family matters." Teachers need to accept their responsibility as perhaps the only people who know what is going on with some children and their families, and as the only advocates a child might have. Teachers need to realize their own legal and moral responsibilities, if they discover their school's policies discourage such active advocacy roles. The Code of Ethics makes it absolutely clear that early childhood professionals have a definite responsibility to act to protect children, and that this responsibility takes precedence over other responsibilities to employers or families (P1.1, Code of Ethics). P1.1 states:

> Above all, we shall not harm children. We shall not participate in practices that are disrespectful, degrading, dangerous, exploitative, intimidating, psychologically damaging, or physically harmful to children. **This principle has precedence over all others in this Code.**

When reports are made, they should include the child's and parents' full names and addresses; the child's age, sex, and birth date; the name and address of the person making the report; and the name, address, and telephone number of the child care center. Professionals should realize that less attention is usually paid to anonymous reports, according to some overworked caseworkers.

Examine Personal Attitudes

Teachers need to examine their own attitudes to be able to work with these families. Many teachers feel great anger toward parents who are hurtful to their small children or expose them to adult violence. It is important to recognize the existence of this anger and to work especially hard to get to know parents and the circumstances of their parenting, in order to develop true empathy for their situations. It is more appropriate for teachers to release some of their negative feelings in conversation with colleagues, rather than with parents, since parents are themselves in need of nurturing and acceptance, not expressions of anger. It is important to remember, however, that confidential material or statements that have not yet been confirmed must be treated professionally.

Create an Atmosphere of Trust and Healing

Teachers' concern and caring for children in these troubled families enable them to support children through very difficult times. It helps these children to know teachers care for them, are dependable and trustworthy, and are concerned enough to help them and their parents. Such an atmosphere of trust may free children to confide their problems and allow them to feel confident in the ability of other adults to help them and their parents. Children need allies in the classroom who can help them provide for their anger to be expressed safely. Play is a vehicle that helps build trust, as teachers accept the children's self-expression. These children do not need to hear condemnation of their angry feelings or of their parents, who are the most important people in their lives no matter how troubled at this time.

Teachers can also comfort themselves in the knowledge that they are providing an important model for children, helping them to realize that not all adults are abusive. All of this is true, whether the children have been abused themselves, or have been witnesses to abuse and violence directed toward someone they love.

Children who have been exposed to violence or neglect have experienced a world in which important adults have not guaranteed their safety and well-being. Coming daily to a classroom with different adults who provide a safe and predictable environment can help them experience security. Classroom teachers need to realize the importance of unvarying routines and gentle limits in helping these children to make sense of their world and make the classroom an emotionally safe place. Teachers need to be careful to alert these children to any changes in the class schedule, discussing any new or different procedures, and preparing them for the presence of new people in the classroom. Teachers should maintain calm and cheerful voices.

Just as young children are particularly vulnerable to the effects of abuse and neglect, even to the alteration of brain development, so too are they capable of **resiliency** and healing, in supportive environments. They need the support and reassurance of caring adults, and tools and activities to allow them to transform their memories of fear and helplessness, choosing symbolic ways to control the ways the adults in their memories act and talk. Healing activities may include imaginative play, art and creative activities, or literary experiences. There are a number of children's books that can help children identify with others' pain and hope for the future. See the list of book suggestions made earlier. The adult's role is not to be that of a play or art therapist; the children are themselves capable of processing their own grief, anger, and fears when in a supportive environment.

Teachers can support children's progress in self-healing activities by posing open-ended questions, such as:

"What happens next?"

"I wonder, what the baby would like to happen differently?"

"What makes your dolly happy?"

Helpful Behaviors for Teachers Who Become Aware of Abuse

- Remain calm and reassuring.
- Listen without judgment, paying close attention.
- Speak with children privately, positioning yourself at eye level.
- Take the child seriously.
- Allow the child to have feelings.
- Reassure the child that abuse is not the child's fault.
- Refrain from using "why" questions.
- Do not condemn the abuser.
- Assure the child that he or she is not alone.
- Tell the truth, and don't make promises you cannot keep.
- Inform the child of process that must be followed to help keep him/her safe.
- Let the child know you are going to help.

Knowing that families may change their abusive patterns with support of community agencies, teachers must be confident that making a report of abuse or neglect is a vital role, and for the good of all involved.